Primary Sources in World History

Wealth, Power, and Inequality

Volume 2, Since 1500

Edited by

James R. Farr and

Patrick J. Hearden

ROWMAN & LITTLEFIELD
Lanham • Boulder • New York • London

Acquisitions Editor: Ashley Dodge
Acquisitions Assistant: Haley White
Sales and Marketing Inquiries: textbooks@rowman.com

Credits and acknowledgments for material borrowed from other sources, and reproduced with permission, appear on the appropriate pages within the text.

Published by Rowman & Littlefield
An imprint of The Rowman & Littlefield Publishing Group, Inc.
4501 Forbes Boulevard, Suite 200, Lanham, Maryland 20706
www.rowman.com

86-90 Paul Street, London EC2A 4NE

British Library Cataloguing in Publication Information Available

Library of Congress Cataloging-in-Publication Data

Names: Farr, James Richard, 1950- editor. | Hearden, Patrick J., 1942- editor.
Title: Primary sources in world history : wealth, power, and inequality / edited by James Farr, Patrick J. Hearden.
Description: Lanham ; Boulder ; New York ; London : Rowman & Littlefield, [2023] | Includes bibliographical references and index. | Contents: Introduction — Document 1. King Hammurabi, The Laws of Hammurabi, ca. 1770 BCE — Document 2. Rameses II and Hattusila III, An Egyptian-Hittite Treaty of Alliance, 1259 BCE — Document 3. Anonymous, A poem reflecting peasant discontent in China, ca. 800 BCE — Document 4. King Ashurbanipal, Assyrian Imperialism, ca. 630 BCE — Document 5. Plutarch, Solon's reforms in Athens, ca. 574 BCE — Document 6. Sun-tzu, The Art of War, ca. 500 BCE — Document 7. Thucydides, The Athenian-Melian Conference, ca 410 BCE — Document 8. Aristotle, Observations on Politics, ca. 350 BCE — Document 9: Ashoka, An Expression of Remorse, ca. 256 BCE — Document 10. Han Feizi, Legalism and the Way of the State in Qin China, ca. 221 BCE — Document 11: Plutarch, A Plan for the Redistribution of Land in the Roman Empire, ca. 133 BCE — Document 12. Free Market or Government Regulation? The Salt and Iron Debates in Han China (81 BCE) — Document 13. Wang Mang, Edict on Land Reform (9 CE) — Document 14. Strabo, A Description of Alexandria, 1st c. CE — Document 15. A Trader's Handbook: The Periplus Maris Erythraei [Guidebook of the Erythraean Sea], c. 50 CE — Document 16. Pliny and Trajan, Letters, c. 111 CE — Document 17. Suetonius, on Octavian Augustus, 121 CE — Document 18. Life, Trade, and Politics along the Silk Roads: the Kharosthi Inscriptions — Document 19. Roman and Persian Accounts of the Capture of the Roman Emperor Valerian in 260 CE — Document 20. The Theodosian Code (438) — Document 21. Priscus Panites, Huns and Romans (c. 450 CE) — Document 22. The Laws of the Salian Franks (507-511) — Document 23. The Institutes of Justinian (533) — Document 24. Corpus Juris Civilis, Justinian on Slavery (533) — Document 25. The Quran, On the Inheritance of Property (610-632) — Document 26. Chinese Tang Emperor Taizong, On Effective Government (648 CE) — Document 27. Tang Legal Code, selections, 653 — Document 28. Charlemagne, Capitularies on the Missi Dominici (802) — Document 29. William I, "the Pious," Foundation Charter of the Monastery at Cluny (910) — Document 30. A Venetian Commenda (1073) — Document 31. Abu Abayd Amr al-Bakri, Book of Highways and of Kingdoms (11th century) — Document 32. Domesday Book, Excerpts (1086) — Document 33. Feudal Contracts, excerpts (1127-1380) — Document 34. Behâ ed-Din, A Muslim View of the Crusades (1191) — Document 35. Anonymous, Observations on Hangzhou, 1235 — Document 36. Marco Polo on Paper Money and the Chinese Economy, c. 1300 — Document 37. Rashid al-Din, Political Influence of Mongol Women, Compendium of Chronicles (Early 14th Century) — Document 38. The Travels of Ibn Battuta (1331) — Document 39. Balduccio Pegolotti, On Overland Trade to China (1310-1340) — Document 40. Parliament of England, An Excerpt from the Statute of Laborers (1351) — Document 41. Ibn Khaldūn on Muslim Traders (1377) — Bibliography — Index — About the authors
Identifiers: LCCN 2022054451 (print) | LCCN 2022054452 (ebook) | ISBN 9781538174357 (v. 1 ; paperback) | ISBN 9781538174371 (v. 2 ; paperback) | ISBN 9781538178638 (cloth) | ISBN 9781538174333 (paperback) | ISBN 9781538174340 (epub) | ISBN 9781538174364 (v. 1 ; epub) | ISBN 9781538174388 (v. 2 ; epub)
Subjects: LCSH: World history—Sources | Economic history—Sources. | World politics—Sources.
Classification: LCC D5 .P74 2023 (print) | LCC D5 (ebook) | DDC 909—dc23/eng/20221115
LC record available at https://lccn.loc.gov/2022054451
LC ebook record available at https://lccn.loc.gov/2022054452

Contents

Introduction

As purposeful actors on the stage of world history, ambitious individuals have exhibited a deep-seated desire to become prosperous and powerful. Their self-interested behavior has led to an ever-changing distribution of wealth and power, both within individual societies and among different political entities such as city-states, kingdoms, nation-states, and empires. Moreover, the expanding supply of goods and services, resulting from technological innovations and scientific discoveries, has led to increasing social, economic, and political inequality around the globe.

This thought-provoking collection of primary documents covers societies in different geographical regions during the last five thousand years. Although comprehensive in scope, this collection focuses on a central theme: the unequal allocation of wealth and power within societies as well as among political entities. The selected documents show that the never-ending quest for wealth and power has led to various forms of inequality. Some, for example, analyze the African slave trade that laid the foundation for the enduring problem of racial inequality in the Americas. Others emphasize the exploitation of peasants, laborers, artisans, farmers, and factory workers that resulted in growing inequality among social classes in every region of the world. Still other documents highlight the widespread existence of gender inequality.

Selected to give students a deeper understanding of how and why inequalities have emerged in societies throughout the world, each document will be introduced by a brief explanation of its historical context. Each of these sources will be followed by a few review questions, giving students an opportunity to test their understanding of the main points.

The sources in this collection reveal that people living at different times and in different places have used similar methods in their drive to achieve similar political and economic objectives. By reflecting uniformities as well as diversities in ideas and actions, these documents undermine assertions of Western intellectual, cultural, or moral superiority. While discarding notions of Western exceptionalism, this collection traces the struggles for wealth and power following the major watersheds that have shaped the contours of world history.

Document 42

The Spanish King's *Requierimento,* 1513

The "Laws of Burgos," promulgated in 1512 in the town of Burgos, Castile, are the first legal code regarding Spanish actions in the Americas, particularly with regard to the Indigenous people of the Americas. They followed the Spanish conquest and colonization of the Americas. Ostensibly they forbade the maltreatment of the Indigenous peoples, and the Spaniards considered the demand for conversion of the Indigenous groups to Christianity a gift to the conquered people. The laws also authorized and legalized the colonial practice of creating *encomiendas*, feudal jurisdictions that the king granted to landlords who were then given the authority to extract tribute and labor services from the Indigenous peoples. They directed Spaniards to read aloud a religious justification and demand for obedience—*El Requierimento* of 1513—supposedly to give Indigenous peoples a chance to submit before being attacked or enslaved. But for peoples who did not speak Spanish, "the requirement" to obey was baffling. The Spanish colonizers continued to enslave them and seize their lands and resources.

On the part of the King, Don Fernando, and of Doña Juana, his daughter, Queen of Castile and León, subduers of the barbarous nations, we their servants notify and make known to you, as best we can, that the Lord our God, living and eternal, created the heaven and the earth, and one man and one woman, of whom you and we, and all the men of the world, were and are all descendants, and all those who come after us. Of all these nations God our Lord gave charge to one man, called St. Peter, that he should be lord and superior of all the men in the world, that all should obey him, and that he should be the head of the whole human race, wherever men should live, and under whatever law, sect, or belief they should be; and he gave him the world for his kingdom and jurisdiction. One of these pontiffs, who succeeded St. Peter

138

as lord of the world in the dignity and seat which I have before mentioned, made donation of these isles and Terra Firma to the aforesaid King and Queen and to their successors, our lords, with all that there are in these territories, Wherefore, as best we can, we ask and require you that you consider what we have said to you, and you take the time that shall be necessary to understand and deliberate upon it, and that you acknowledge the Church as the ruler and superior of the whole world, But if you do not do this, and maliciously make delay in it, I certify to you that, with the help of God, we shall power-fully enter into your country, and shall make war against you in all ways and manners that we can, and shall subject you to the yoke and obedience of the Church and of their highnesses; we shall take you, and your wives, and your children, and shall make slaves of them, and as such shall sell and dispose of them as their highnesses may command; and we shall take away your goods, and shall do you all the mischief and damage that we can, as to vassals who do not obey, and refuse to receive their lord, and resist and contradict him: and we protest that the deaths and losses which shall accrue from this are your fault, and not that of their highnesses, or ours, nor of these cavaliers [knights] who come with us.

Source: Copyright, US National Library of Medicine; public domain.

REVIEW QUESTIONS

Why does the king demand the acceptance by the Indians of the *Requieri-mento?* How is it justified?

What would happen to the Indians if they refused to accept it?

Document 43

Jacob Fugger's Letter to Holy Roman Emperor Charles V, 1523

Great international financial houses, such as the German House of Fugger, rose with the growth of wealth in Europe in the sixteenth century. The head of the Fugger firm, Jacob, used the company's resources for both economic and political objectives, placing wealth in the service of power. The House of Fugger became the greatest financier to the royal Habsburg family. The following letter written in 1523 from Jacob to Charles V, head of the House of Hapsburg, Holy Roman Emperor, King of Spain, and the most powerful ruler in Europe, reminds the emperor of the financial assistance Fugger provided Charles to be elected Holy Roman Emperor in 1519 by the electoral princes of Germany rather than his competitor Francis I of France.

Your Imperial Majesty doubtless knows how I and my kinsmen have ever hitherto been disposed to serve the House of Austria in all loyalty to the furtherance of its well-being and prosperity; wherefore, in order to be pleasing to Your Majesty's Grandsire, the late Emperor Maximilian, and to gain for Your Majesty the Roman Crown, we have held ourselves bounden to engage ourselves towards divers princes who placed their Trust and Reliance upon myself and perchance on No Man besides. We have, moreover, advanced to Your Majesty's Agents for the same end a Great Sum of Money, of which we ourselves have had to raise a large part from our Friends. It is well known that Your Imperial Majesty could not have gained the Roman Crown save with mine aid, and I can prove the same by the writings of Your Majesty's Agents given by their own hands. In this matter I have not studied mine own Profit. For had I left the House of Austria and had been minded to further France, I had obtained much money and property, such as was then offered to me. How grave a Disadvantage had in this case accrued to Your Majesty and the House of Austria, Your Majesty's Royal Mind well knoweth.

Source: Richard Ehrenberg, Ca*pital and Finance in the Age of the Renaissance: A Study of the Fuggers and Their Connections*, trans. H. M. Lucas (New York: Augustus M. Kelley, 1963), 80.

REVIEW QUESTIONS

What do you think Fugger sent this letter?

Does it contain a veiled threat to the emperor?

Document 44

A Spaniard's Account of Aztec Tribute. Gonzalo Fernandez de Oviedo y Valdes, *Aztec Tribute*, 1526

When the Aztecs conquered their neighboring city-states in central Mexico between 1420 and 1480, they took control of a tribute system that previous empires, notably the Toltec, had established. We have no written evidence for this system before the conquest by the Spanish in 1521, but a Spanish observer, Gonzalo Fernandez de Oviedo y Valdés (1478–1557), described the system in a long chronicle completed in 1526, *La historia general y natural de las Indias*, about the Spanish colonization of their new American empire. Bartolomé de las Casas, a contemporary of Oviedo and likewise an observer and historian of New Spain, challenged the veracity of much of Oviedo's account.

. . . .

The Indians of New Spain, I have been told by reliable persons who gained their information from Spaniards who fought with Hernando Cortes in the conquest of that land, are the poorest of the many nations that live in the Indies at the present time. In their homes they have no furnishings or clothing other than the poor garments which they wear on their persons, one or two stones for grinding maize, some pots in which to cook the maize, and a sleeping mat. Their meals consist chiefly of vegetables cooked with chili, and bread. They eat little—not that they would not eat more if they could get it, for the soil is very fertile and yields bountiful harvests, but the common people and plebeians suffer under the tyranny of their Indian lords, who tax away the greater part of their produce in a manner that I shall describe. Only the lords and their relatives, and some principal men and merchants, have estates and lands of their own; they sell and gamble with their lands as they please, and they sow and harvest them but pay no tribute. Nor is any tribute paid by artisans, such as masons, carpenters, feather-workers, or silversmiths, or by singers and kettle-drummers (for every Indian lord has musicians in his household, each according to his station). But such persons render personal service when it is required, and none of them is paid for his labor.

Each Indian lord assigns to the common folk who come from other parts of the country to settle on his land (and to those who are already settled there) specific fields, that each may know the land that he is to sow. And the majority of them have their homes on their land; and between twenty and thirty, or forty and fifty houses have over them an Indian head who is called tiquitlato, which in the Castilian tongue means "the finder (or seeker) of tribute." At harvest time this tiquitlato, inspects the cornfield and observes what each one reaps, and when the reaping is done they show him the harvest, and he counts the ears of corn that each has reaped, and the number of wives and children that each of the vassals in his charge possesses. And with the harvest before him he calculates how many ears of corn each person in that household will require till the next harvest, and these he gives to the Indian head of that house; and he does the same with the other produce, namely kidney beans, which are a kind of small beans, and chili, which is their pepper; and chia, which is as fine as mustard seed, and which in warm weather they drink, ground and made into a solution in water and used for medicine, roasted and ground; and cocoa, which is a kind of almond that they use as money, and which they grind, make into a solution, and drink; and cotton, in those places where it is raised, which is in the hot lands and not the cold; and pulque, which is their wine; and all the various products obtained from the maguey plant, from which they obtain food and drink and footwear and clothing. This plant grows in the cold regions, and the leaves resemble those of the cinnamon tree, but are much larger. Of all these and other products they leave the vassal only enough to sustain him for a year. And in addition the vassal must earn enough to pay the tribute of mantles, gold, silver, honey, wax, lime, wood, or whatever products it is customary to pay as tribute in that country. They pay this tribute every forty, sixty, seventy, or ninety days, according to the terms of the agreement. This tribute also the tiquitlato receives and carries to his Indian lord. Ten days before the close of the sixty or hundred days, or whatever is the period appointed for the payment of tribute, they take to the house of the Indian lord the produce brought by the tiquitlatos; and if some poor Indian should prove unable to pay his share of tribute, whether for reasons of health or poverty, or lack of work, the tiquitlato tells the lord that such-and-such will not pay the proportion of the tribute that had been assigned to him; then the lord tells the tiquitlato to take the recalcitrant vassal to a tianguez or market, which they hold every five days in all the towns of the land, and there sell him into slavery, applying the proceeds of the sale to the payment of his tribute. . . .

All the towns have their own lands, long ago assigned for the provision of the orchilobos or ques or temples where they kept their idols; and these lands were and are the best of all. And they have this custom: At seeding time all would go forth at the summons of the town council to sow these fields, and to weed them at the proper time, and to cultivate the grain and harvest it and carry it to a house in which lived the pope and the teupisques, piaches, exputhles and piltautles (or, as we would say, the bishops, archbishops, and the canons and prebendaries, and even choristers, for each major temple had these five classes of officials). And they supported themselves from this harvest, and the Indians also raised chickens for them to eat. In all the towns Montezuma had his designated lands, which they sowed for him in the same way as the temple lands; and if no garrison was stationed in their towns, they would carry the crops on their backs to the great city of Temistitan [Tenochtitlán]; but in the garrison towns the grain was eaten by Montezuma's soldiers, and if the town did not sow the land, it had to supply the garrison with food, and also give them chickens and all other needful provisions.

Source: Benjamin Keen, ed. and trans., *Latin American Civilization*, 3rd ed. (Boston: Houghton Mifflin, 1974), I:19–22.

REVIEW QUESTIONS

If the land the author described was so fertile and productive, why did the cultivators remain in poverty?

What was a *tiquitlato*, and what role did he play in the tribute system described here?

Can you reconstruct the hierarchical nature of Aztec society from this document?

Document 45

Ogier Ghiselin de Busbecq, *On Süleyman the Lawgiver*, ca. 1530

Ogier Ghiselin de Busbecq (1522–1592) was the Austrian ambassador to the Ottoman Empire through most of the 1550s. He collected his extensive correspondence and published his Turkish Letters late in his life. Ghiselin de Busbecq's ambassadorship coincided with the reign of the Ottoman Sultan Süleyman (r. 1520–1566), referred to as "the Magnificent" or "the Lawgiver." Süleyman's rule marked the apogee of Ottoman power. He expanded the empire through unrelenting military campaigns, gaining control of Hungary (but failing to take Vienna), and displacing the Persian Safavids from Baghdad. Although he absorbed conquered territories and their resources, the costs of war outpaced the new revenues. So he expanded an increasingly elaborate financial bureaucracy for more effective tax collection to pay for his army. Süleyman reformed imperial administration, but the institutionalization of a bureaucracy eventually was dominated by viziers, high-ranking political advisors and ministers. Vast wealth accumulated in the hands of this administrative hierarchy. Süleyman consciously proclaimed his sovereignty by building grand royal palaces and mosques and lavishly patronizing court poets and painters.

The Sultan [Süleyman "The Lawgiver"] was seated on a very low ottoman, not more than a foot from the ground, which was covered with a quantity of costly rugs and cushions of exquisite workmanship; near him lay his bow and arrows. . . . The Sultan then listened to what I had to say; but the language I used was not at all to his taste, for the demands of his Majesty breathed a spirit of independence and dignity, which was by no means acceptable to one who deemed that his wish was law; and so he made no answer beyond saying in an impatient way, "Giusel, giusel," that is, "well, well." After this we were dismissed to our quarters.

The Sultan's hall was crowded with people, among whom were several officers of high rank. Besides these, there were all the troopers of the Imperial guard, and a large force of Janissaries [the elite infantry corps], but there was not in all that great assembly a single man who owed his position to anything save his valor and his merit. No distinction is attached to birth among the Turks; the respect to be paid to a man is measured by the position he holds in the public service. There is no fighting for precedence; a man's place is marked out by the duties he discharges. . . . It is by merit that men rise in the service, a system which ensures that posts should only be assigned to the competent. Each man in Turkey carries in his own hand his ancestry and his position in life, which he may make or mar as he will. Those who receive the highest offices from the Sultan are for the most part the sons of shepherds or herdsmen, and so far from being ashamed of their parentage, they actually glory in it, and consider it a matter of boasting that they owe nothing to the accident of birth; for they do not believe that high qualities are either natural or hereditary, nor do they think that they can be handed down from father to son, but that they are partly the gift of God, and partly the result of good training, great industry, and unwearied zeal; arguing that high qualities do not descend from a father to his son or heir, any more than a talent for music, mathematics, or the like. . . . Among the Turks, therefore, honors, high posts, and judgeships are the rewards of great ability and good service. If a man is dishonest, or lazy, or careless, he remains at the bottom of the ladder, an object of contempt; for such qualities there are no honors in Turkey!

This is the reason that they are successful in their undertakings, that they lord it over others, and are daily extending the bounds of their empire. These are not our ideas, with us there is no opening left for merit; birth is the standard for everything; the prestige of birth is the sole key to advancement in the public service.

The Turkish monarch going to war takes with him over 40,000 camels and nearly as many baggage mules, of which a great part, when he is invading Persia, are loaded with rice and other kinds of grain. These mules and camels also serve to carry tents and armor, and likewise tools and munitions for the campaign. . . . The invading army carefully abstains from encroaching on its supplies at the outset, as they are well aware that, when the season for campaigning draws to a close, they will have to retreat over districts wasted by the enemy, or scraped as bare by countless hordes of men and droves of baggage animals, as if they had been devastated by locusts; accordingly they reserve their stores as much as possible for this emergency. . . .

From this you will see that it is the patience, self-denial, and thrift of the Turkish soldier that enable him to face the most trying circumstances, and come safely out of the dangers that surround him. What a contrast to our men! . . .

For each man is his own worst enemy, and has no foe more deadly than his own intemperance, which is sure to kill him, if the enemy be not quick. It makes me shudder to think of what the result of a struggle between such different systems must be; one of us must prevail and the other be destroyed, at any rate we cannot both exist in safety. On their side is the vast wealth of their empire, unimpaired resources, experience and practice in arms, a veteran soldiery, an uninterrupted series of victories, readiness to endure hardships, union, order, discipline, thrift, and watchfulness. On ours are found an empty exchequer, luxurious habits, exhausted resources, broken spirits, a raw and insubordinate soldiery, and greedy generals; there is no regard for discipline, license runs riot, the men indulge in drunkenness and debauchery, and, worst of all, the enemy are accustomed to victory, we, to defeat. Can we doubt what the result must be?

Source: C. T. Foster and F. H. Blackburne Daniell, "Süleyman the Lawgiver," in *The Life and Letters of Ogier Ghiselin de Busbecq* (London: Hakluyt Society, 1881), 1:152–56.

REVIEW QUESTIONS

What does Süleyman's reception of Ghiselin de Busbecq suggest about his attitude toward the ambassador?

What does Ghiselin de Busbecq claim about the roles of merit, effort, and honor in Ottoman society? Do you believe he is a trustworthy and accurate observer? Why or why not?

What is Ghiselin de Busbecq's implied message for his European readers?

Document 46

Pedro de Cieza de Leon, *Chronicles of the Incas*, 1553 CE

The Spaniards under Francisco Pizarro conquered the Inca Empire in 1531. Upon reading about the far-off land of the Incas, sixteen-year-old Pedro de Cieza de Leon left Spain for his first expedition to the New World in 1532. He spent most of the following two decades as a soldier, explorer, and administrator in regions stretching south from what is now Colombia, along the west coast of South America. Particularly when he was in Ecuador and Peru between 1548 and 1550, he kept extensive written records. When he returned to Seville in 1551, he started preparing his *Chronicle of Peru* for publication. The first volume was published in 1553; Cieza de Leon died in 1554, and subsequent volumes were published posthumously.

In the time of the Yncas there was a royal road made by the force and labour of men, which began at this city of Quito, and went as far as Cuzco, whence another of equal grandeur and magnitude led to the provinces of Chile, which is more than one thousand two hundred leagues from Quito. On these roads there were pleasant and beautiful lodgings and palaces every three or four leagues, very richly adorned. These roads may be compared to that which the Romans made in Spain, and which we call the silver road. . . .

The distance from the city of Quito to the palaces of Tumebamba is fifty-three leagues. Soon after leaving the city there is a village called Pansaleo, the natives of which differ in some things from their neighbors, especially in the fillets or bands round their heads; for by these bands the descent of the Indians is known, and the provinces of which they are natives.

These and all the other natives of the kingdom, over a space of more than one thousand two hundred leagues, speak the general language of the Yncas, being that which is used in Cuzco. They generally speak this language, because such is the order of the Yncas, and it was a law throughout the kingdom that this language should be used. Fathers were punished if they neglected to teach it to their sons in childhood, yet, notwithstanding that they speak the language of Cuzco, all these tribes had a language of their own which was spoken by their ancestors. . . .

A little beyond Mulahalo are the village and great building called Llactu-cunga, which were as important as those of Quito. The buildings, though now in ruins, give signs of their former grandeur, and in some of the walls the niches may be seen where the golden sheep and other valuable things which they carved, were kept. The buildings set apart for the Kings Yncas, and the temple of the sun, where they performed their sacrifices and supersti-tions, were especially remarkable for these precious things. There were also many virgins here, dedicated to the service of the temple, whom they called Mama-cuna. In this village the Lords Yncas placed a superintendent, who had charge of the collection of tribute in the neighboring provinces, and stored it here, where there were also a great number of Mitimaes. The Yncas, consid-ering that the centre of their dominion was the city of Cuzco, whence they promulgated laws, and sent forth their captains to war, and that Quito was six hundred leagues distant, while the road to Chile was still longer; and consid-ering, also, that all of this vast extent of country was peopled by barbarous, and some of them very warlike tribes, they adopted the following system in order to keep the empire in greater security. It was first commenced in the time of King Ynca Yupanqui, father of the great Tupac Ynca Yupanqui, and grandfather of Huayna Ccapac.

As soon as a province was conquered, ten or twelve thousand men were ordered to go there with their wives, but they were always sent to a country where the climate resembled that from which they came. If they were natives of a cold province, they were sent to a cold one; and if they came from a warm province, they were sent to a warm one. These people were called Mitamaes, which means Indians who have come from one country and gone to another. They received grants of land on which to work, and sites on which to build their houses. The Yncas decreed that these Mitamaes should always obey the orders of the governors and captains who were placed over them, so that if the natives rebelled, the Mitimaes, who owed obedience to their captains, would punish them and force them into the service of the Yncas; consequently, if there was any disturbance among the Mitimaes themselves, they were at-tacked by the natives. By this policy these Lords Yncas kept their empire safe and free from rebellion; and the provinces were well supplied with provi-sions, for most of the inhabitants of each were natives of some other country. They also adopted another plan, in order that they might not be detested by the natives. They never deprived the native caciques of their inheritance, and if any one of them was so guilty as to merit deprivation, the vacant office was given to this sons or brothers, and all men were ordered to obey them.

Source: Clements R. Markham, trans. and ed., *The Travels of Pedro de Cieza de Leon, A.D. 1532–1550, Contained in the First Part of his Chronicle of Peru* (London: Hakluyt Society, 1864), 144–50.

REVIEW QUESTIONS

How did Incan linguistic policies and relocations strengthen the unity of empire and help prevent rebellion against royal rule?

Describe the structure of the Inca bureaucracy. How effective was it in administering government across the large territory of the Incan Empire?

What seems to be Cieza de Leon's attitude toward the Inca? What, if anything, does he seem to find admirable about Inca society, and what, if anything, does he seem to find disturbing?

Document 47

Russian Tsar Ivan IV, Grant to the Stroganovs to Colonize Siberia, 1558

In 1477, the Muscovite ruler Ivan III conquered the important trading city of Novgorod to capture the valuable fur trade that channeled through it that was destined for European markets. Fur exports became the regime's chief source of imported silver, and Russia's rulers were unrelenting in their search for the valuable resource. This pushed Russian expansion into Siberia, and Russia's first great imperial thrust eastward was spearheaded by Ivan IV (1530–1584). He brought the Volga River under Russian control, which opened trade with China, the Safavid Empire in Persia, and the Mughal Empire in India. The conquest also opened lands to peasant migration, bringing under cultivation steppe land that had been formerly grazed by pastoral nomads. The tsar authorized the colonizers' ruthless treatment of the Indigenous peoples. This charter from Tsar Ivan IV to Grigorii Stroganov demonstrates the imperial interest in the colonization and economic benefits of Siberia.

I, Tsar and Grand Prince of All Russia Ivan Vasil'evich, have bestowed my favor upon Grigorii, son of Anika Stroganov, [and] have allowed him to found a settlement [gorodok] in that uninhabited region eighty-eight versty below Perm' the Great along the Kama River . . . on the state forest land downstream on both banks of the Kama to the Chusovaia River, wherever there is a strong and safe place; and I have ordered him to place cannon and harquebuses in the settlement, and to install cannoneers, harquebusiers, and gate sentries [vorotniki] for protection against the Nagai and against other hordes, and to cut down the forest near that settlement along the rivers and around the lakes and up to the sources [of the rivers], and to plow the plowland around that settlement, and to establish homesteads, and to invite into that settlement such men as are not listed in the registry books [nepismennye] and bear the tiaglo [state duties levied upon peasants in cash, kind, and labor]. . . . And if any men should come to that settlement from our state or from other lands with money or with goods, to buy salt or fish or other goods, these men shall be free to sell their goods here and to buy from them without any imposts. And if any men should come from Perm' to live, Grigorii [Stroganov] shall receive [only] those men who have been discharged [from their community] and are not listed in the registry books and do not bear the tiaglo. And if any salt deposits should be found in this region, he shall establish salterns there and boil salt. And they may catch fish in the rivers and lakes of this region without paying a tax. And if silver or copper or lead deposits should be found anywhere, Grigorii shall straightway report to our treasurers about these deposits, and he shall not work these deposits himself without our knowledge. . . . And I have granted him [these] privileges for twenty years.

Source: G. F. Miller [Mueller], *Storiia Sibiri* (Moscow: AN SSSR, 1937–1941), 1: 333.

REVIEW QUESTIONS

What benefits does the tsar anticipate from granting this charter to Grigorii Stroganov?

What incentives does the tsar offer Stroganov to colonize Siberia?

How might have the effects of this charter impacted Indigenous peoples of Siberia?

Document 48

A Spaniard's View of the Columbian Exchange, 1590

Alfred W. Crosby Jr. coined the term "Columbian exchange" referring to the global redistribution of plants, animals, and diseases that began in the sixteenth century following the initial contacts among European colonizers, Africans, and the Indigenous peoples of the Americas. José de Acosta was a Spanish Jesuit missionary and naturalist, and his scientific and historical work *Natural and Moral History of the Indies* (1590) describes the New World in terms of agricultural production and the unique flora of the Americas and, in the excerpt here, discusses the "exchange" referred to by Crosby.

The Indies have been better repaid in the matter of plants than in any other kind of merchandise; for those few that have been carried from the Indies into Spain do badly there, whereas the many that have come over from Spain prosper in their new homes. I do not know whether to attribute this to the excellence of the plants that go from here or to the bounty of the soil over there. Nearly every good thing grown in Spain is found there; in some regions they do better than in others. They include wheat, barley, garden produce and greens and vegetables of all kinds, such as lettuce, cabbage, radishes, onions, garlic, parsley, turnips, carrots, eggplants, endive, salt-wort, spinach, chickpeas, beans, and lentils—in short, whatever grows well here, for those who have gone to the Indies have been careful to take with them seeds of every description. . . .

The trees that have fared best there are the orange, lemon, citron, and others of that sort. In some parts there are already whole forests and groves of orange trees. Marveling at this, I asked on a certain island who had planted so many orange trees in the fields. To which they replied that it might have happened that some oranges fell to the ground and rotted, whereupon the seeds germinated, and, some being borne by the waters to different parts, gave rise to these dense groves. This seemed a likely reason. I said before that orange trees have generally done well in the Indies, for nowhere have I found a place where oranges were not to be found; this is because everywhere in the Indies the soil is hot and humid, which is what this tree most needs. It does not grow in the highlands; oranges are transported there from the valleys or the coast. The orange preserve which is made in the islands is the best I have ever seen, here or there.

Peaches and apricots also have done well, although the latter have fared better in New Spain. . . . Apples and pears are grown, but in moderate yields; plums give sparingly; figs are abundant, chiefly in Peru. Quinces are found everywhere, and in New Spain they are so plentiful that we received fifty choice ones for half a real. Pomegranates are found in abundance, but they are all sweet, for the people do not like the sharp variety. The melons are very good in some regions, as in Tierra Firme and Peru. Cherries, both wild and cultivated, have not so far prospered in the Indies. . . . In conclusion, I find that hardly any of the finer fruits is lacking in those parts. As for nuts, they have no acorns or chestnuts, nor, as far as I know, have any been grown over there until now. Almonds grow there, but sparingly. Almonds, walnuts, and filberts are shipped there from Spain for the tables of epicures.

By profitable plants I mean those plants which not only yield fruit but bring money to their owners. The most important of these is the vine, which gives wine, vinegar, grapes, raisins, verjuice, and syrup—but the wine is the chief concern. Wine and grapes are not products of the islands or of Tierra Firme; in New Spain there are vines which bear grapes but do not yield wine. The reason must be that the grapes do not ripen completely because of the rains which come in July and August and hinder their ripening; they are good only for eating. Wine is shipped from Spain and the Canary Islands to all parts of the Indies, except Peru and Chile, where they have vineyards and make very good wine. This industry is expanding continually, not only because of the goodness of the soil, but because they have a better knowledge of winemaking.

The vineyards of Peru are commonly found in warm valleys where they have water channels; they are watered by hand, because rain never falls in the coastal plains, and the rains in the mountains do not come at the proper time. . . . The vineyards have increased so far that because of them the tithes of the churches are now five and six times what they were twenty years ago. The valleys most fertile in vines are Victor, near Arequipa; Yca, hard by Lima; and Caracaro, close to Chuquiavo. The wine that is made there is shipped to Potosi and Cuzco and various other parts, and it is sold in great quantities, because since it is produced so abundantly it sells at five or six ducats the jug, or arroba, whereas Spanish wine (which always arrives with the fleets) sells for ten and twelve. . . . The wine trade is no small affair, but does not exceed the limits of the province.

The silk which is made in New Spain goes to other provinces—to Peru, for example. There was no silk industry before the Spaniards came; the mulberry trees were brought from Spain, and they grow well, especially in the province called Misteca, where they raise silkworms and make good taffetas; they do not yet make damasks, satins, or velvets, however.

The sugar industry is even wider in scope, for the sugar not only is consumed in the Indies but is shipped in quantity to Spain. Sugar cane grows remarkably well in various parts of the Indies. In the islands, in Mexico, in Peru, and elsewhere they have built sugar mills that do a large business. I was told that the Nasca [Peru] sugar mill earned more than thirty thousand pesos a year. The mill at Chicama, near Trujillo [Peru], was also a big enterprise, and those of New Spain are no smaller, for the consumption of sugar and preserves in the Indies is simply fantastic. From the island of Santo Domingo, in the fleet in which I came, they brought eight hundred and ninety-eight chests and boxes of sugar. I happened to see the sugar loaded at the port of Puerto Rico, and it seemed to me that each box must contain eight arrobas. The sugar industry is the principal business of those islands—such a taste have men developed for sweets!

Olives and olive trees are also found in the Indies, in Mexico, and in Peru, but up to now they have not set up any mills to make olive oil. Actually, it is not made at all, for they prefer to eat the olives, seasoning them well. They find it unprofitable to make olive oil, and so all their oil comes from Spain.

Source: Jose de Acosta, *Natural and Moral History of the Indies* (London: Hakluyt Society, 1880).

REVIEW QUESTIONS

According to Acosta, what impact did the Spanish have on the Indies?

Do you see evidence of the "Columbian Exchange" described by the historian Alfred Crosby?

What crops were the most profitable in the Americas, and why?

Document 49

Eskander Bey Monshi, *Biography of Shah Abbas I*, ca. 1600

Under the Safavid Dynasty, Persia was the sole Middle Eastern power able to meet the Ottomans on equal terms, and the two great Islamic states were often in conflict. Persia was Shiite in its religious orientation, whereas the Ottomans adhered to the Sunni variety of Islam. The most outstanding Safavid Emperor was Shah Abbas the Great (1588–1629), whose capital at Isfahan was fabled to be one of the wealthiest and most beautiful cities of the East. A portrait of Shah Abbas emerges in the biography of him written by his secretary, Eskander Bey Monshi (1560–1632?).

On Shah 'Abbas's Justice, Concern for the Security of the Roads, and Concern for the Welfare of His Subjects

The greater part of governing is the preservation of stability within the kingdom and security on the roads. Prior to the accession of Shah 'Abbas, this peace and security had disappeared in Iran, and it had become extremely difficult for people to travel about the country. As soon as he came to the throne, Shah 'Abbas turned his attention to this problem. He called for the principal highway robbers in each province to be identified, and he then set about eliminating this class of people. Within a short space of time, most of their leaders had been arrested. Some of them, who had been driven by misfortune to adopt this way of life, were pardoned by Shah 'Abbas and their troubles solved by various forms of royal favor. Overwhelmed by this display of royal clemency, these men swore to serve the king and to behave as law-abiding citizens. Others, however, were handed over to the sahna (a police official) for punishment, and society was rid of this scourge. With security restored to the roads, merchants and tradesmen traveled to and from the Safavid Empire.

The welfare of his people was always a prime concern of the Shah, and he was at pains to see that the people enjoyed peace and security, and that oppression by officialdom, the major cause of anxiety on the part of the common man, was totally stamped out in his kingdom. Substantial reductions were made in the taxes due to the di van: first, the tax on flocks in Iraq, amounting to nearly fifteen thousand Iraqi toman, was remitted to the people of that province, and the population of Iraq, which is the flourishing heart of Iran and the seat of government, by this gift was preferred above the other provinces. Second, all di van levies were waived for all Shi'ites throughout the empire during the month of Ramadan. The total revenues for one month, which according to the computation of the di van officials amounted to some twenty thousand toman, were given to the people as alms. The object was that they should be free from demands for taxes during this blessed month, which is a time to be devoted to the service and worship of God. . . .

On Shah 'Abbas's Policy-making and Administration

If scholars consider Sha 'Abbas to be the founder of the laws of the realm and an example in this regard to the princes of the world, they have justification for this opinion, for he has been responsible for some weighty legislation in the field of administration.

One of his principal pieces of legislation has been his reform of the army. Because the rivalries of the qezelbas tribes had led them to commit all sorts of enormities, and because their devotion to the Safavid royal house had been weakened by dissension, Shah 'Abbas decided (as the result of divine inspiration, which is vouchsafed to kings but not to ordinary mortals), to admit into the armed forces groups other than the qezelbas. He enrolled in the armed forces large numbers of Georgian, Circassian, and other golams, and created the office of qollar-aqasi commander-in-chief of the golam regiments), which had not previously existed under the Safavid regime. Several thousand men were drafted into regiments of musketeers from the Cagatay tribe, and from various Arab and Persian tribes in Khorasan, Azerbaijan, and Tabarestan. Into the regiments of musketeers, too, were drafted all the riff-fall from every province—sturdy, serviceable men who were unemployed and preyed on the lower classes of society. By this means the lower classes were given relief from their lawless activities, and the recruits made amends for their past sins by performing useful service in the army. All these men were placed on the golam muster rolls. Without question, they were an essential element in 'Abbas' conquests, and their employment had many advantages.

Shah 'Abbas tightened up provincial administration. Any emir or noble who was awarded a provincial governorship, or who was charged with the security of the highways, received his office on the understanding that he discharge his duties in a proper manner. If any merchant or traveler or resident were robbed, it was the duty of the governor to recover his money for him or replace it out of his own funds. This rule was enforced throughout the Safavid Empire. As a result, property was secure, and people could travel without hindrance to and from Iran.

Another of Shah 'Abbas' policies has been to demand a truthful reply whenever he asked anyone for information. Lying, he said, is forbidden and considered a sin by God, so why should it not be a sin to lie to him who is one's king, one's spiritual director, and one's benefactor? Is not falsehood to such a one ingratitude? In the opinion of Shah 'Abbas, lying to one's benefactor constituted the rankest ingratitude. If he detected anyone in a lie, he visited punishment upon him. The effects of this policy have been felt at all levels of society. For example, if someone has committed various acts that merit the death penalty and the king questions him on his conduct, the poor wretch has no option but to tell the truth. In fact, the opinion is commonly held that, if a person tells a lie to the Shah, the latter intuitively knows he is lying. The result is that the biggest scoundrel alive hesitates to allow even a small element of falsehood to creep into any story he is telling the Shah. The beneficial effects of this on government and the administration of justice need no elaboration. . . .

On His Simplicity of Life, Lack of Ceremony, and Some Contrary Qualities

The character of the Shah contains some contradictions; for instance, his fiery temper, his imperiousness, his majesty, and regal splendor are matched by his mildness, leniency, his ascetic way of life, and his immortality. His is equally at home on the dervish's mat and the royal throne. When he is in good temper, he mixes with the greatest informality with the members of his household, his close friends and retainers with others, and treats them like brothers. In contrast, when he is in a towering rage, his aspect is so terrifying that the same man who, shortly before, was his boon companion and was treated with all the informality of a close friend, dares not to speak a word out of turn for fear of being accused of insolence or discourtesy. At such times, the emirs, sultans, and even the court wits and his boon companions keep silent, for fear of the consequences. The Shah, then, possesses these two contrasting natures, each of which is developed to the last degree. . . .

On Shah 'Abbas's Concern for the Rights of His Servants and His Avoiding Laying Hands on Their Possessions

One of the most agreeable qualities of this monarch is his compassionate treatment of his servants, which is coupled with a concern that faithful service should receive its just reward. His record in this regard is so outstanding that it is not matched by that of any other chivalrous prince. As long as his servants are constant in their loyalty, the royal favor is lavished upon them, nor is it withdrawn for any trifling offense committed out of ignorance or from negligence. If any of his servants dies from natural causes, or gives his life in battle in the defense of the faith and the state, the Shah is generous in his treatment of their dependents. In the case of officeholders, even if their sons are too young at the time of their father's death to be fit for office, nevertheless, in order to resuscitate their families, he confers the same office on the sons out of his natural generosity and magnanimity.

Moreover, since the Shah considers the possessions and treasures of this world of little value, even if the deceased has left substantial sums of money, such is the Shah's magnanimity and concern to follow the prescripts of canon law that he (unlike the majority of princes) does not lay covetous eyes on the inheritance, but divides it among the heirs in the proportions ordained by God. This is regarded by some as his most praiseworthy characteristic, for most of the princes of the world consider it impossible for them to show greater appreciation for their servants than by following this practice, which brings with it heavenly rewards. . . .

On Shah 'Abbas's Breadth of Vision, and His Knowledge of World Affairs and of the Classes of Society

After he has dealt with the affairs of state, Shah 'Abbas habitually relaxes. He has always been fond of conviviality and, since he is still a young man, he enjoys wine and the company of women. But this does not affect the scrupulous discharge of his duties, and he knows in minute detail what is going on in Iran and also in the world outside. He has a well-developed intelligence system, with the result that no one, even if he is sitting at home with his family, can express opinions which should not be expressed without running the risk of their being reported to the Shah. This has actually happened on numerous occasions.

As regards his knowledge of the outside world, he possesses information about the rulers (both Muslim and non-Muslim) of other countries, about the size and composition of their armies, about their religious faith and the organization of their kingdoms, about their highway systems, and about the prosperity or otherwise of their realms. He has cultivated diplomatic relations with most of the princes of the world, and the rulers of the most distant parts of Europe, Russia, and India are on friendly terms with him. Foreign ambassadors bearing gifts are never absent from his court, and the Shah's achievements in the field of foreign relations exceed those of his predecessors.

Shah 'Abbas mixes freely with all classes of society, and in most cases is able to converse with people in their own particular idiom. He is well versed in Persian poetry; he understands it well, indulges in poetic license, and sometimes utters verses himself. He is a skilled musician, an outstanding composer of rounds, rhapsodies, and part-songs; some of his compositions are famous. As a conversationalist, he is capable of elegant and witty speech.

Source: Roger M. Savory, trans., *Eskander Bey Monshi: History of Shah Abbas the Great* (Boulder, CO: Westview Press, 1978), 1:523, 527–29, 531, 533. Copyright © 1978 Roger M. Savory. This work is protected by copyright and the making of this copy was with the permission of Access Copyright. Any alteration of its content or further copying in any form whatsoever is strictly prohibited unless otherwise permitted by law.

REVIEW QUESTIONS

What does this description of Shah 'Abbas suggest about what qualities and virtues were valued in Safavid society?

Why is honesty held to be such an important trait?

Does this description seem reliable to you? Is there anything here that suggests Shah 'Abbas might have some negative attributes or behaviors? Does the author provide sufficient evidence to convince you that he is representing Shah 'Abbas accurately?

Document 50

Huo Ju-hsia, From a Memorandum on the Portuguese in Macao, Seventeenth Century

Portuguese merchants entered the established trading networks of the Indian Ocean and the South China Sea in the sixteenth century, seeking to access the riches of the east, especially spices, and to channel them to European markets for substantial profits. Their strategy was to employ military force to seize the choke points of the Indian Ocean trading system, a region that for centuries had been politically fragmented and relatively violence-free in its trading relations. The Portuguese sought to consolidate their gains behind fortresses built astride the key chokepoints. They first came to Macau on the south coast of China (across the Pearl River Delta from present-day Hong Kong) in 1557. The Chinese government of the Ming Dynasty permitted the Portuguese to establish a permanent settlement in Macao for an annual rent payable in silver but to remain under Chinese authority and sovereignty (it remained a Portuguese territory until 1999). The Chinese did not trade directly with Japan, so although the Portuguese were granted only limited privileges of self-governance, they were, in turn, permitted to trade from this port with Japan as well as India and other parts of China. The Portuguese became invaluable middlemen, shuttling Japanese silver to China and Chinese silks to Japan. The following memorandum by a seventeenth-century Chinese official expresses Chinese concerns about the newcomers and how to deal with them.

There is a vast difference between peaceful trade and piratical raids. To be unable to pacify the barbarians [the Portuguese] who have come from afar to partake of our civilization is a reflection on our own goodness. To criticize them for their shortcomings while only too gladly collecting taxes from them is not what a righteous man should do. Without making any effort to observe their conduct or to differentiate the law-abiding from the evildoers, we indiscriminately call all of them bandits. Once we have branded them as bandits, we are obligated to exterminate them—only to see more of them come. Is this policy really wise? What then should we do?

There are three measures we can take, each exclusive of the others. The best measure would be to govern them in the same manner as we govern our own people: to convert the territory they have occupied into a subprefecture and to place them under the jurisdictional control of duly appointed government officials. The next best measure would be to expel them and make sure that they never come back again. The worst measure would be to cut off their food supply, which would force them to revolt, and then use armed forces to exterminate them.

Ironical though it may seem, the best way to carry out the first measure is to threaten them with the adoption of the second. The government should issue an order addressed to them as follows: "It is reported by military authorities that you have gathered hooligans around yourselves and equipped yourselves with horses and cannons. We are afraid that some unprincipled, avaricious Chinese may incite you to illegal activities which will do harm to local communities. Therefore we have ordered the armed forces to demolish your dwellings and send you back to where you came from, to avoid trouble for all parties." While proclaiming this order, we should alert our troops for action. If the barbarians obey the order, they will leave China for other countries, where they are welcome to do whatever damage they choose. If on the other hand they beg us to let them stay and declare that they have no objection to being subject to Chinese administration, we should petition the imperial government to build cities for them and to govern them with Chinese officials. From then on they will be subject to Chinese law. This is the way barbarians have been transformed into Chinese; it is by far the best course to follow.

Some people may say that once these barbarians are expelled from China, there will be no further disturbances on our frontier and our people will be much better off. How, they may ask, can expulsion be regarded as the second best course? I reply that to have confidence in the barbarians' natural goodness for our own defense is reflective of the greatness of the Son of Heaven, that to welcome all barbarians to partake of our civilization is indicative of the benign nature of the Celestial King, and that to provide food for our enemy so as to pacify the frontier betokens the farsightedness of a powerful nation. Besides, there are also practical considerations: (1) For the past hundred years the yearly revenue derived from overseas trade has been as large as the total revenue of a first-rate subprefecture, and this revenue has been used to support the armed forces in the Liangkwang region [Kwangtung and Kwangsi]. If this trade is cut off, where can we find funds to meet the military demand? (2) Macao has proved to be an effective buffer for

Hsiangshan. Because it is there, pirates like Lao wan, Tseng Yi-pen, and Ho Ya-pa have not dared to launch attacks, and the whole area has remained peaceful as a result. If the barbarians in Macao are expelled, Hsiangshan will have to defend itself. In short, to construct cities for them and to govern them with Chinese officials in accordance with the Chinese law will be the best policy to follow. It is best because it is a policy of kindness by which peace can be secured without great effort.

Source: *China in Transition, 1517–1911*, Dan J. Li, trans. (New York: Van Nostrand Reinhold Company, 1969), 6–7. Reprinted by permission of Wadsworth Publishing Company.

REVIEW QUESTIONS

What characteristics does the author ascribe to the Portuguese? Why does he refer to them as "piratical" and "bandits"?

What options does the author think the Chinese have in dealing with the Portuguese?

What does he think would be the best policy? Why?

Document 51

Muscovite Merchants Complaints to the Russian Tsar Alexis I about English Traders, 1646, and the Tsar's Response in His Decree on English Merchants, 1649

English and Dutch merchants had been trading in Russia for years before 1646, but in that year, the Russian merchants of several Muscovite towns submitted a complaint to the Tsar Alexis I about the commercial practices of the Europeans, singling out especially the English merchants. The tsar responded to them with a decree against the English, but cited political as much as economic reasons for his decree.

Muscovite Merchants Complaints to the Russian Tsar about English Traders

To the tsar and grand prince of all Russia Aleksei Mikhailovich, your slaves and orphans, Sire, the humble gosti and the lowly trading men of the gostinaia sotnia, the sukonnaia sotnia, and the chernye sotni make petition. . . .

Our complaint, Sire, is against the foreigners, the English and the Dutch merchants and those of Brabant and of Hamburg, who come to Moscow to trade.

The English merchants now come to the Muscovite state in parties of sixty or seventy or more; and they have built and bought for themselves many yards and warehouses in the town of Archangel and in Kholmogory, in Vologda, in Iaroslavl', in Moscow, and in other towns; and they have built mansions and cellars of stone; and now they remain in the Muscovite state without leaving, just as in their own country; and they no longer sell their wares to Russians or barter them for Russian wares in the town of Archangel but take their various wares to Moscow and to other towns themselves; and as soon as certain goods become expensive, they begin to sell those goods; but as for goods that are cheaper and not in demand, they keep those goods in their warehouses for two or three years, and when the price of those goods goes up, then they start selling them. And the Russian wares in the Muscovite state, which we, your slaves and orphans, used to exchange for their wares, they are now buying up themselves, conspiring among each other; and they send [Russian men] to make purchases in the towns and in the countryside, having concluded loan agreements and made debtors out of many poor and indebted Russians; and the Russians buy those goods and bring them to [the foreigners], and they take them out to their country without paying customs duties . . . and they cheat you out of your customs duties, Sire; and all the trade that we, your slaves and orphans, have carried on from time immemorial has been seized by the English foreigners; and as a result of this we, your slaves and orphans, have been deprived of our ancient trading pursuits, carried on from time immemorial, and we no longer journey to Archangel. And not only, Sire, have those foreigners left us, your slaves and orphans, without a livelihood, but they have reduced the entire Muscovite state to starvation, buying up meat and grain and all kinds of provisions in Moscow and other towns, Sire, and taking them out of the Muscovite state to their own country.

The Decree Concerning Restrictions on English Merchants, June 1, 1649

The sovereign tsar and grand prince Aleksei Mikhailovich of all Russia has decreed, and the boyars have resolved, that you Englishmen [must] betake yourselves beyond the seas with all your possessions; and that, to trade in all kinds of goods with the trading men of the Muscovite state, you may come from beyond the seas to the town of Archangel, but that you may not journey to Moscow and to other towns, either with or without merchandise. . . .

And you Englishmen are being prohibited from remaining in the Muscovite state for this reason: heretofore you carried on your trade in the Muscovite state on the strength of the sovereign's charters, which had been granted to you at the request of your sovereign, the English king Charles [I], out of brotherly friendship and love. But now it has become known to our great sovereign, His Majesty the tsar, that the entire English nation has committed a most evil deed, putting to death their sovereign, King Charles; and on account of that evil deed you have been prohibited from remaining in the Muscovite state.

And you Englishmen should heed the decree of His Majesty the tsar and should betake yourselves from the Muscovite state beyond the seas, with all your possessions.

Source: *A Sourcebook for Russian History from Early Times to 1917*. Vol. 1,
Early Times to the Late Seventeenth Century, ed. George Vernadsky, et al.
(New Haven: Yale University Press, 1972), 246–47.

REVIEW QUESTIONS

What activities of the English merchants most alarm the muscovite merchants? Why?

What is the tsar's response? Does he have political and economic motivations?

Document 52

Tokugawa Iemitsu, Injunctions to Peasants, 1649

In contrast to the chaos of the Warring States period that preceded it, Japan's Tokugawa Shogunate was characterized by intense governmental regulation of nearly all aspects of life. Feudal hierarchies were strictly enforced. Peasants were taxed heavily throughout the Tokugawa Shogunate; Tokugawa Iemitsu (r. 1623–1651) set the tax rate on rice at 50 percent of production. Over time, this high tax rate changed peasant behavior because not only did it lead to frequent peasant protests into the eighteenth century, but many peasants also ironically increased their productivity. The amount of rice owed as tax was fixed regardless of any particular year's yield, so farmers who succeeded in raising their output were able to keep 100 percent of the surplus. The fixed quantity of rice due also meant that peasants paid an even higher effective tax rate in years of drought or other poor growing conditions—a hardship that, in turn, led to more peasant protests. The following are the injunctions to the peasants decreed in 1649 by Iemitsu.

— Farm work must be done with the greatest diligence. Planting must be neat, all weeds must be removed, and on the borders of both wet and dry fields beans or similar foodstuffs are to be grown, however small the space.
— Peasants must rise early and cut grasses before cultivating the fields. In the evening they are to make straw rope or straw bags, all such work to be done with great care.
— They must not buy tea or saké to drink, nor must their wives.
— Men must plant bamboo or trees round the farmhouse and must use the fallen leaves for fuel so as to save expense.
— Peasants are people without sense or forethought. Therefore they must not give rice to their wives and children at harvest time, but must

save food for the future. They should eat millet, vegetables, and other coarse food instead of rice. Even the fallen leaves of plants should be saved as food against famine. . . . During the seasons of planting and harvesting, however, when the labour is arduous, the food taken may be a little better than usual.

— The husband must work in the fields, the wife must work at the loom. Both must do night work. However good-looking a wife may be, if she neglects her household duties by drinking tea or sightseeing or rambling on the hillsides, she must be divorced.

— Peasants must wear only cotton or hemp—no silk. They may not smoke tobacco. It is harmful to health, it takes up time, and costs money. It also creates a risk of fire.

Source: Sir George Bailey Sansom, *A History of Japan* (Stanford, CA: Stanford University Press, 1963), III:99.

REVIEW QUESTIONS

Why do you think the peasants are forbidden to drink both tea and saké?

What do these injunctions suggest about gender roles under the Tokugawa Shogunate?

Why does the Shogun claim that "Peasants are people without sense or forethought"?

Document 53

John Keymer, *On Dutch Trade and Commerce,* Early Seventeenth Century

Despite engagement in a war of Independence with Spain from 1568 to 1648, the Dutch Republic (formally declared the independent United Provinces in 1578) emerged as a dominant economic power in Europe in the early seventeenth century. Other European powers took notice. An Englishman named John Keymer published a series of works, urging changes in English economic policies, some in direct response to Dutch practices. In one, *Observations Touching Trade and Commerce with the Hollanders, and Other Nations,* incorrectly attributed to Sir Walter Raleigh and that is excerpted here, he articulated what he perceived as Dutch advantages in trade over England. It was addressed to King James I of England (r. 1603–1625).

May it please your most Excellent Majesty
I have diligently, in my travels, observed how the countries herein mentioned [mainly Holland] do grow potent with abundance of all things to serve themselves and other nations, where nothing groweth; and that their never-dryed fountains of wealth, by which they raise their estate to such an admirable height, [so] that they are . . . [now] a wonder to the world, [come] from your Majesty's seas and lands.

I thus moved, began to dive into the depth of their policies and circumventing practices, whereby they drain, and still covet to exhaust, the wealth and coin of this kingdom, and so with our own commodities to weaken us, and finally beat us quite out of trading in other countries. I found that they more fully obtained these their purposes by their convenient privileges, and settled constitutions, than England with all the laws, and superabundance of home-bred commodities which God hath [be stowed on] your sea and land. . . .

To bring this to pass they have many advantages of us; the one is, by their fashioned ships called boyers, hoy-barks, boys, and others [the famous fluytschips whose innovative design enlarged the cargo hold and reduced the deck area] that are made to hold great bulk of merchandise, and to sail with a few men for profit. For example, . . . [Dutch ships] do serve the merchant better cheap by one hundred pounds [English money] in his freight than we can, by reason he hath but nine or ten mariners, and we near thirty; thus he saveth twenty men's meat and wages in a voyage; and so in all other their ships according to their burden, by which means they are freighted wheresoever they come, to great profit, whilst our ships lie still and decay. . . .

Of this their smallness of custom [duty, or taxes] inwards and outwards, we have daily experience; for if two English ships, or two of any other nations be at Bourdeaux [a French port, exporting mainly wine], both laden with wine of three hundred tons apiece, the one bound for Holland . . . , the other for England, the merchant shall pay about nine hundred pounds custom here, and other duties, when the other in Holland . . . shall be cleared for less than fifty pounds, and so in all other wares and merchandizes accordingly, which draws all nations to traffick with them; and although it seems but small duties which they receive, yet the multitudes of all kind of commodities and coin that is brought in by themselves and others, and carried out by themselves and others, is so great, that they receive more custom and duties to the state, by the greatness of their commerce in one year, than England doth in two years. . . .

And if it happen that a trade be stopped by any foreign nation, which they heretofore usually had, or hear of any good trading which they never had, they will hinder others, and seek either by favour, money, or force, to open the gap of traffick for advancement of trade amongst themselves, and employment of their people.

And when there is a new course or trade erected, they give free custom inwards and outwards, for the better maintenance of navigation, and encouragement of the people to that business.

Thus they and others glean the wealth and strength from us to themselves; and these reasons following procure them this advantage of us.

1. The merchant[s] which maketh all things in abundance, by reason of their storehouses continually replenished with all kind of commodities.
2. The liberty of free traffick for strangers to buy and sell in Holland, and other countries and states, as if they were free-born, maketh great intercourse.
3. The small duties levied upon merchants, draws all nations to trade with them.
4. Their fashioned ships continually freighted before ours, by reason of their few mariners and great bulk, serving the merchant cheap.
5. Their forwardness to further all manner of trading.
6. Their wonderful employment of their busses [herring boats] for fishing, and the great returns they make.
7. Their giving free custom inwards and outwards, for any new-erected trade, by means whereof they have gotten already almost the sole trade into their hands. . . .

The merchandises of France, Portugal, Spain, Italy, Turkey, East and West Indies, are transported most by the Hollanders, and other petty states, into the east and northeast kingdoms of [Europe] . . . and the merchandises brought from the last-mentioned . . . , being wonderful many, are likewise by the Hollanders and other petty states most transported into the southern and western dominions, and yet the situation of England lieth far better for a storehouse to serve the southeast and northeast regions than theirs doth, and hath far better means to do it, if we will bend our course for it.

No sooner a dearth of fish, wine, or corn here, and other merchandise, but forthwith the Emdeners, Hamburghers [from the German ports of Emden and Hamburg], and Hollanders, out of their storehouses, [load] fifty or one hundred ships, or more, dispersing themselves round about this kingdom, and carry away great store of coin and wealth for little commodity, in those times of dearth; by which means they suck our commonwealth of her riches, cut down our merchants, and decay our navigation; not with their natural commodities, which grow in their own countries, but the merchandises of other countries and kingdoms.

Therefore it is far more easy to serve ourselves, hold up our merchants, and increase our ships and mariners, and strengthen the kingdom; and not only keep our money in our own realm, which other nations still rob us of, but bring in theirs who carry ours away, and make the bank or coin a storehouse to serve other nations as well, and far better cheap than they. . . .

The abundance of corn [wheat] groweth in the east kingdoms [of Europe], but the great storehouses for grain to serve Christendom, and heathen countries in the time of dearth, is in the Low-Countries [Holland and modernday Belgium], wherewith, upon every occasion of scarcity and dearth they do inrich themselves seven years after, employ their people, and get great freights for their ships in other countries, and we not one in that course.

The mighty vineyards and store of salt is in France and Spain; but the great vintage and staple of salt is in the Low-Countries, and they send near one thousand sail of ships with salt and wine only into the east kingdoms yearly, besides other places, and we not one in that course.

The exceeding groves of wood are in the east kingdoms, but the huge piles of [lumber] . . . and timber, is in the Low-Countries, where none grow, wherewith they serve themselves and other parts, and this kingdom with those commodities; they have five or six hundred great long ships continually using that trade, and we none in that course.

The wool, cloth, lead, tin, and divers other commodities, are in England; but by means of our wool and cloth going out rough, undress'd, and undy'd, there is an exceeding manufactory and drapery in the Low-Countries, wherewith they serve themselves and other nations, and advance greatly the employment of their people at home, and traffick abroad, and put down ours in foreign parts, where our merchants trade unto, with our own commodities. . . .

The Low-Countries send into the east kingdoms yearly, about three thousand ships, trading into every city and port-town, taking the advantage, and vending their commodities to exceeding profit, and buying and lading their ships with plenty of those commodities, which they have from every of those towns 20 per cent cheaper than we, by reason of the difference of the coin, and their fish yields ready money, which greatly advanceth their traffick, and decayeth ours.

Source: *Observation Touching on the Trade and Commerce with the Hollanders, and Other Nations* (London: William Sheeres, 1653). Reprinted in *Sources of the Western Tradition*, 4th ed., eds. Marvin Perry, Joseph R. Peden and Theodore H. Von Laue (Boston: Houghton Mifflin), 1:341–43.

REVIEW QUESTIONS

How did innovation in ship design affect the profitability of Dutch trade?

How does the author explain how money flows out of England and into the Dutch Republic?

What do you think the author perceived as the greatest economic advantages the Dutch held over England?

Document 54

Thomas Mun, *England's Treasure by Foreign Trade*, 1664

Thomas Mun (1571–1641) was born into a successful London merchant family. Like many merchants of their day, the Mun family traded in high-value commodities such as spices, dyestuffs, and silks, which were purchased with gold and silver bullion from other traders in markets far removed from Britain. Mun's stepfather was a member of the powerful English East India Company (chartered by Queen Elizabeth I in 1600), as was one of his elder brothers. Mun appears to have traded for a time in the Mediterranean, but in 1615 he became a director of the East India Company. His first economic writings in the 1620s, when a severe depression in trade raised commodity prices, were a defense of overseas trade in general and of the East India Company in particular. He continued to serve the East India Company until his death. *England's Treasure*, addressed to his son, was probably written in 1630 but was not published until 1664. It repeated many of Mun's arguments on the balance of trade and the ways in which a nation slowly increased its wealth. Mun's work was influential for more than a century after his death and served as a central reference point for Adam Smith (author of *The Wealth of Nations* in 1776), who regarded it as the classic statement of mercantilist doctrine. Mercantilism, the theory that a nation's prosperity depended on the maintenance of a favorable balance of trade, dominated economic thought for decades. These ideas did not change significantly until Smith proposed the notion that free, not managed, trade created wealth.

The Qualities which are required in a perfect Merchant of Forraign Trade

The love and service of our Countrey consisteth not so much in the knowledge of those duties which are to be performed by others, as in the skilful practice of that which is done by our selves; and therefore (my Son) it is now fit that I say something of the Merchant, which I hope in due time shall be thy Vocation: Yet herein are my thoughts free from all Ambition, although I rank thee in a place of so high estimation; for the Merchant is worthily called The Steward of the Kingdoms Stock, by way of Commerce with other Nations; a work of no less Reputation than Trust, which ought to be performed with great skill and conscience, that so the private gain may ever accompany the publique good. And because the nobleness of this Profession may the better stir up thy desires and endeavours to obtain those abilities which may effect it worthily, I will briefly set down the excellent qualities which are required in a perfect Merchant.

1. He ought to be a good Penman, a good Arithmetician, and a good Ac-comptant, by that noble order of Debtor and Creditor, which is used onely amongst Merchants; also to be expert in the order and form of Charter-parties, Bills of Lading, Invoyces, Contracts, Bills of Ex-change, and Policies of Ensurance.

2. He ought to know the Measures, Weights, and Monies of all forraign Countries, especially where we have Trade, & the Monies not onely by their several denominations, but also by their intrinsique values in weight & fineness, compared with the Standard of this Kingdom, without which he cannot well direct his affaires.

3. He ought to know the Customs, Tolls, Taxes, Impositions, Conducts and other charges upon all manner of Merchandize exported or im-ported to and from the said Forraign Countries.

4. He ought to know in what several commodities each Countrey abounds, and what be the wares which they want, and how and from whence they are furnished with the same.

5. He ought to understand, and to be a diligent observer of the rates of Exchanges by Bills, from one State to another, whereby he may the better direct his affairs, and remit over and receive home his Monies to the most advantage possible.

6. He ought to know what goods are prohibited to be exported or im-ported in the said forraign Countreys, lest otherwise he should incur great danger and loss in the ordering of his affairs.

7. He ought to know upon what rates and conditions to fraight his Ships, and ensure his adventures from one Countrey to another, and to be well acquainted with the laws, orders and customes of the Ensurance office both here and beyond the Seas, in the many accidents which may hap-pen upon the damage or loss of Ships or goods, or both these.

8. He ought to have knowledge in the goodness and in the prices of all the several materials which are required for the building and repairing of Ships, and the divers workmanships of the same, as also for the Masts, Tackling, Cordage, Ordnance, Victuals, Munition, and Provisions of many kinds; together with the ordinary wages of Commanders, Officers, and Mariners, all which concern the Merchant as he is an Owner of Ships.

9. He ought (by the divers occasions which happen sometimes in the buying and selling of one commodity and sometimes in another) to have indifferent if not perfect knowledge in all manner of Merchandize or wares, which is to be as it were a man of all occupations and trades.

10. He ought by his voyaging on the Seas to become skilful in the Art of Navigation.

11. He ought, as he is a Traveller, and sometimes abiding in forraign Countreys, to attain to the speaking of divers Languages, and to be a diligent observer of the ordinary Revenues and expences of forraign Princes, together with their strength both by Sea and Land, their laws, customes, policies, manners, religions, arts, and the like; to be able to give account thereof in all occasions for the good of his Countrey.

12. Lastly, although there be no necessity that such a Merchant should be a great Scholar; yet is it (at least) required, that in his youth he learn the Latine tongue, which will the better enable him in all the rest of his endeavours.

The means to enrich this Kingdom, and to encrease our Treasure

Although a Kingdom may be enriched by gifts received, or by purchase taken from some other Nations, yet these are things uncertain and of small consideration when they happen. The ordinary means therefore to increase our wealth and treasure is by Forraign Trade, wherein wee must ever observe this rule; to sell more to strangers yearly than wee consume of theirs in value. For suppose that when this Kingdom is plentifully served with the Cloth, Lead, Tinn, Iron, Fish and other native commodities, we doe yearly export the overplus to forraign Countreys to the value of twenty two hundred thousand pounds; by which means we are enabled beyond the Seas to buy and bring in forraign wares for our use and Consumptions, to the value of twenty hundred thousand pounds: By this order duly kept in our trading, we may rest assured that the Kingdom shall be enriched yearly two hundred thousand pounds, which must be brought to us in so much Treasure; because that part of our stock which is not returned to us in wares must necessarily be brought home in treasure.

The Exportation of our Moneys in Trade of Merchandize is a means to encrease our Treasure

This Position is so contrary to the common opinion, that it will require many and strong arguments to prove it before it can be accepted of the Multitude, who bitterly exclaim when they see any monies carried out of the Realm; affirming thereupon that wee have absolutely lost so much Treasure, and that this is an act directly against the long continued laws made and confirmed by the wisdom of this Kingdom in the High Court of Parliament, and that many places, nay Spain it self which is the Fountain of Mony, forbids the exportation thereof, some cases only excepted.

First, I will take that for granted which no man of judgement will deny, that we have no other means to get Treasure but by forraign trade, for Mines wee have none which do afford it, and how this mony is gotten in the managing of our said Trade I have already shewed, that it is done by making our commodities which are exported yearly to over ballance in value the forraign wares which we consume; so that it resteth only to shew how our moneys may be added to our commodities, and being jointly exported may so much the more encrease our Treasure.

Wee have already supposed our yearly consumptions of forraign wares to be for the value of twenty hundred thousand pounds, and our exportations to exceed that two hundred thousand pounds, which sum wee have thereupon affirmed is brought to us in treasure to ballance the accompt. But now if we add three hundred thousand pounds more in ready mony unto our former exportations in wares, what profit can we have (will some men say) although by this means we should bring in so much ready mony more than wee did before, seeing that wee have carried out the like value.

To this the answer is, that when wee have prepared our exportations of wares, and sent out as much of everything as wee can spare or vent abroad: It is not therefore said that then we should add our money thereunto to fetch in the more mony immediately, but rather first to enlarge our trade by enabling us to bring in more forraign wares, which being sent out again will in due time much encrease our Treasure.

For although in this manner wee do yearly multiply our importations to the maintenance of more Shipping and Mariners, improvement of His Majesties Customs and other benefits: yet our consumption of those forraign wares is no more than it was before; so that all the said encrease of commodities brought in by the means of our ready mony sent out as is afore written, doth in the end become an exportation unto us of a far greater value than our said moneys were.

The answer is (keeping our first ground) that if our consumption of forraign wares be no more yearly than is already supposed, and that our exportations be so mightily encreased by this manner of Trading with ready money, as is before declared: It is not then possible but that all the over ballance or difference should return either in mony or in such wares as we must export again, which, as is already plainly shewed will be still a greater means to encrease our Treasure.

For it is in the stock of the Kingdom as in the estates of private men, who having store of wares, does not therefore say that they will not venture out or trade with their mony (for this were ridiculous) but do also turn that into wares, whereby they multiply their Mony, and so by a continual and orderly change of one into the other grow rich, and when they please turn all their estates into Treasure; for they that have Wares cannot want mony.

Neither is it said that Mony is the Life of Trade, as if it could not subsist without the same; for we know that there was great trading by way of commutation or barter when there was little mony stirring in the world. The Italians and some other Nations have such remedies against this want, that it can neither decay nor hinder their trade, for they transfer bills of debt, and have Banks both publick and private, wherein they do assign their credits from one to another daily for very great sums with ease and satisfaction by writings only, whilst in the mean time the Mass of Treasure which gave foundation to these credits is employed in Forraign Trade as a Merchandize, and by the said means they have little other use of money in those countreys more than for their ordinary expences. It is not therefore the keeping of our mony in the Kingdom, but the necessity and use of our wares in forraign Countries, and our want of their commodities that causeth the vent and consumption of all sides, which makes a quick and ample Trade. If wee were once poor, and now having gained some store of mony by trade with resolution to keep it still in the Realm; shall this cause other Nations to spend more of our commodities than formerly they have done, whereby we might say that our trade is Quickned and Enlarged? no verily, it will produce no such good effect: but rather according to the alteration of times by their true causes wee may expect the contrary; for all men do consent that plenty of mony in a Kingdom doth make the native commodities dearer, which as it is to the profit of some private men in their revenues, so is it directly against the benefit of the Publique in the quantity of the trade; for as plenty of mony makes wares dearer, so dear wares decline their use and consumption.

There is yet an objection or two as weak as all the rest: that is, if wee trade with our Mony wee shall issue out the less wares; as if a man should say, those Countreys which heretofore had occasion to consume our Cloth, Lead, Tin, Iron, Fish, and the like, shall now make use of our monies in the place of those necessaries, which were most absurd to affirm, or that the Merchant had not rather carry out wares by which there is ever some gains expected, than to export mony which is still but the same without any encrease.

But on the contrary there are many Countreys which may yield us very profitable trade for our mony, which otherwise afford us no trade at all, because they have no use of our wares, as namely the East Indies for one in the first beginning thereof, although since by industry in our commerce with those Nations we have brought them into the use of much of our Lead, Cloth, Tin, and other things, which is a good addition to the former vent of our commodities.

Again, some men have alleged that those Countries which permit mony to be carried out, do it because they have few or no wares to trade withall: but wee have great store of commodities, and therefore their action ought not to be our example.

To this the answer is briefly, that if we have such a quantity of wares as doth fully provide us of all things needful from beyond the seas: why should we then doubt that our monys sent out in trade, must not necessarily come back again in treasure; together with the great gains which it may procure in such manner as is before set down? And on the other side, if those Nations which send out their monies do it because they have but few wares of their own, how come they then to have so much Treasure as we ever see in those places which suffer it freely to be exported at all times and by whomsoever? I answer, Even by trading with their Moneys; for by what other means can they get it, having no Mines of Gold or Silver?

Thus may we plainly see, that when this weighty business is duly considered in his end, as all our humane actions ought well to be weighed, it is found much contrary to that which most men esteem thereof, because they search no further than the beginning of the work, which misinforms their judgments, and leads them into error: For if we only behold the actions of the husbandman in the seed-time when he casteth away much good corn into the ground, we will rather accompt him a mad man than a husbandman: but when we consider his labours in the harvest which is the end of his endeavours, we find the worth and plentiful encrease of his actions.

Source: Thomas Mun, *England's Treasure by Forraign Trade* (Macmillan and Company, 1895). Public Domain.

REVIEW QUESTIONS

According to Mun, what are the qualities and skills a merchant should culti-vate? How do those compare with what would be considered good business skills today?

How does Mun defend his argument against critics who accuse the East India Company of spending more in gold and silver than it gained in return? Why does he think that his plan will increase the country's wealth in the long term?

In what way does this excerpt exemplify the principles of mercantilism? Con-sider how Mun defines "treasure" and what he sees as the goal of foreign trade.

English Bill of Rights, 1689

The English parliament was a political body representing the interests of land-owning families that comprised about 2 percent of the population. Traditionally, English kings and queens needed the consent of parliament to levy taxes, establishing a principle about property that monarchs could not take it from their subjects without their consent. When King James I (r. 1603–1625) and Charles I (r. 1625–1649) challenged this right in the early and mid-seventeenth century, a civil war erupted (1642–1649). The Glorious Revolution of 1688–1689 was a political settlement that transformed England. It ended the civil wars that had devastated the country and placed the crown of England on the heads of the Protestant Dutchman William of Orange and his English wife Mary Stuart, daughter of the deposed Catholic king James II (r. 1685–1688). The English Bill of Rights, excerpted here, was enacted as statutory law by the Parliament on December 16, 1689. It restates the Declaration of Right that Parliament had presented to William and Mary in February 1689 as conditions they must accept to become joint sovereigns of England.

An Act Declaring the Rights and Liberties of the Subject and Settling the Succession of the Crown

Whereas the Lords Spiritual and Temporal and Commons assembled at Westminster, lawfully, fully and freely representing all the estates of the people of this realm, did upon the thirteenth day of February in the year of our Lord one thousand six hundred eighty-eight [old style date] present unto their Majesties, then called and known by the names and style of William and Mary, prince and princess of Orange, being present in their proper persons, a certain declaration in writing made by the said Lords and Commons in the words following, viz.:

. . . .

And whereas the said late King James the Second having abdicated the government and the throne being thereby vacant, his Highness the prince of Orange (whom it hath pleased Almighty God to make the glorious instrument of delivering this kingdom from popery and arbitrary power) did (by the advice of the Lords Spiritual and Temporal and divers principal persons of the Commons) cause letters to be written to the Lords Spiritual and Temporal being Protestants, and other letters to the several counties, cities, universities, boroughs and cinque ports, for the choosing of such persons to represent them as were of right to be sent to Parliament, to meet and sit at Westminster upon the two and twentieth day of January in this year one thousand six hundred eighty and eight [old style date], in order to such an establishment as that their religion, laws and liberties might not again be in danger of being subverted, upon which letters elections having been accordingly made;

And thereupon the said Lords Spiritual and Temporal and Commons, pursuant to their respective letters and elections, being now assembled in a full and free representative of this nation, taking into their most serious consideration the best means for attaining the ends aforesaid, do in the first place (as their ancestors in like case have usually done) for the vindicating and asserting their ancient rights and liberties declare;

That the pretended power of suspending the laws or the execution of laws by regal authority without consent of Parliament is illegal;

That the pretended power of dispensing with laws or the execution of laws by regal authority, as it hath been assumed and exercised of late, is illegal;

. . . .

That levying money for or to the use of the Crown by pretence of prerogative, without grant of Parliament, for longer time, or in other manner than the same is or shall be granted, is illegal;

. . . .

That the raising or keeping a standing army within the kingdom in time of peace, unless it be with consent of Parliament, is against law;

. . . .

That election of members of Parliament ought to be free;

That the freedom of speech and debates or proceedings in Parliament ought not to be impeached or questioned in any court or place out of Parliament;

That excessive bail ought not to be required, nor excessive fines imposed, nor cruel and unusual punishments inflicted;

That jurors ought to be duly impanelled and returned, and jurors which pass upon men in trials for high treason ought to be freeholders;

That all grants and promises of fines and forfeitures of particular persons before conviction are illegal and void;

And that for redress of all grievances, and for the amending, strengthening and preserving of the laws, Parliaments ought to be held frequently.

And they do claim, demand and insist upon all and singular the premises as their undoubted rights and liberties, and that no declarations, judgments, doings or proceedings to the prejudice of the people in any of the said premises ought in any wise to be drawn hereafter into consequence or example; to which demand of their rights they are particularly encouraged by the declaration of his Highness the prince of Orange as being the only means for obtaining a full redress and remedy therein. Having therefore an entire confidence that his said Highness the prince of Orange will perfect the deliverance so far advanced by him, and will still preserve them from the violation of their rights which they have here asserted, and from all other attempts upon their religion, rights and liberties, the said Lords Spiritual and Temporal and Commons assembled at Westminster do resolve that William and Mary, prince and princess of Orange, be and be declared king and queen of England, France and Ireland and the dominions thereunto belonging, to hold the crown and royal dignity of the said kingdoms and dominions to them, the said prince and princess, during their lives and the life of the survivor to them, and that the sole and full exercise of the regal power be only in and executed by the said prince of Orange in the names of the said prince and princess during their joint lives, and after their deceases the said crown and royal dignity of the same kingdoms and dominions to be to the heirs of the body of the said princess, and for default of such issue to the Princess Anne of Denmark and the heirs of her body, and for default of such issue to the heirs of the body of the said prince of Orange. And the Lords Spiritual and Temporal and Commons do pray the said prince and princess to accept the same accordingly. . . .

Upon which their said Majesties did accept the crown and royal dignity of the kingdoms of England, France and Ireland, and the dominions thereunto belonging, according to the resolution and desire of the said Lords and Commons contained in the said declaration. And thereupon their Majesties were pleased that the said Lords Spiritual and Temporal and Commons, being the two Houses of Parliament, should continue to sit, and with their Majesties' royal concurrence make effectual provision for the settlement of the religion, laws and liberties of this kingdom, so that the same for the future might not be in danger again of being subverted, to which the said Lords Spiritual and Temporal and Commons did agree, and proceed to act accordingly. Now in pursuance of the premises the said Lords Spiritual and Temporal and Commons in Parliament assembled, for the ratifying, confirming and establishing the said declaration and the articles, clauses, matters and things therein contained by the force of law made in due form by authority of Parliament, do pray that it may be declared and enacted that all and singular the rights and liberties asserted and claimed in the said declaration are the true, ancient and indubitable rights and liberties of the people of this kingdom, and so shall be esteemed, allowed, adjudged, deemed and taken to be; and that all and every the particulars aforesaid shall be firmly and strictly holden and observed as they are expressed in the said declaration, and all officers and ministers whatsoever shall serve their Majesties and their successors according to the same in all time to come.

Source: Bill of Rights, UK Parliament, 1689. Also, The Avalon Project: Documents in Law, History and Diplomacy, Yale Law School, © 2008 Lillian Goldman Law Library, 127 Wall Street, New Haven, CT 06511.

REVIEW QUESTIONS

What "religion, rights, and liberties" is Parliament seeking to protect in this document? What supreme authority does parliament claim for itself?

On what conditions do the new monarchs, William and Mary, accept the crown of England?

Document 56

On Slavery and the Slave Trade: Letters from the Kings of the Kongo to the King of Portugal, 1526; A European Account of the Slave Trade, Seventeenth Century; Malachy Postelthwayt, *The National and Private Advantages of the African Trade Considered*, 1746; A Virginian planter's view of slavery, 1757

These documents provide varying perspectives on slavery and the slave trade from the sixteenth to the eighteenth centuries. The first is a letter from Mvemba a Nzinga (who converted to Christianity and was baptized with the name Afonso), King of the Kongo, to the kings of Portugal. The Kongo was a wealthy kingdom that controlled extensive trading networks and vast territory in west central Africa, including parts of what is now Angola, the Republic of the Congo, and the Democratic Republic of the Congo. Mvemba a Nzinga defeated a half-brother in a conflict over succession in 1506, and he attributed his victory to both Portuguese weapons and a miraculous Christian vision. He corresponded extensively with the rulers of Portugal about the administration of church and state, as well as on matters of trade, including slavery. In the seventeenth century, the Dutch and English entered the West African slave trade, supplanting the Portuguese as the principal traders in the Atlantic economy. Dealing in slaves was a profitable business that attracted numerous entrepreneurs. The second document is a seventeenth-century account of conditions of the captured slaves by one such slave trader. The last two documents by Malachy Postelthwayt (a respected writer of works on commerce) and the Virginia planter Peter Fontaine, date from the eighteenth century and both emphasize the economic benefits of slavery to the planters in the American colonies and to Great Britain. They were not exceptional in their defense of slavery.

Mvemba a Nzinga (King Afonso I), *Letters to Kings Manuel I and Joao III of Portugal*, 1506–1526

Effects of Portuguese Trade (1526)

Lord,

[Y]our factors and officials give to the men and merchants that come to this Kingdom . . . and spread . . . so that many vassals owing us obedience . . . rebel because they have more goods [through trade with Portuguese] than us, who before had been content and subject to our . . . jurisdiction, which causes great damage. . . .

And each day these merchants take our citizens, native to the land and children of our nobles and vassals, and our relations, because they are thieves and men of bad conscience, steal them with the desire to have things of this kingdom . . . take them to sell. . . . Our land is all spoiled . . . which is not to your service. . . . For this we have no more necessity for other than priests and educators, but [send] no more merchandise . . . nor merchants. . . .

Expansion and Regulation of the Slave Trade (1526)

[M]any of our subjects, through the desire for merchandise and things of this Kingdom which you bring . . . to satisfy their appetite, steal many of our free and exempt subjects. And nobles and their children and our relatives are often stolen to be sold to white men . . . hidden by night. . . . And the said white men are so powerful . . . they embark and . . . buy them, for which we want justice, restoring them to liberty. . . .

And to avoid this great evil, by law all white men in our kingdom who buy slaves . . . must make it known to three nobles and officials of our court. . . .

A European Slave Trader, *An account of the Slave Trade*, Seventeenth Century

When our slaves were come to the seaside, our canoes were ready to carry them off to the longboat, if the sea permitted, and she convey'd them aboard ship, where the men were all put in irons, two and two shackled together, to prevent their mutiny, or swimming ashore.

The negroes are so wilful and loth to leave their own country, that they have often leap'd out of the canoes, boat and ship, into the sea, and kept under water till they were drowned, to avoid being taken up and saved by our boats, which pursued them; they having a more dreadful apprehension of Barbadoes than we can have of hell, tho' in reality they live much better there than in their own country; but home is home, etc: we have likewise seen divers of them eaten by the sharks, of which a prodigious number kept about the ships in this place, and I have been told will follow her hence to Barbadoes, for the dead negroes that are thrown over-board in the passage. I am certain in our voyage there we did not want the sight of some every day, bur that they were the same I can't affirm.

We had about 12 negroes did wilfully drown themselves, and others starv'd themselves to death; for 'tis their belief that when they die they return home to their own country and friends again.

I have been inform'd that some commanders have cut off the legs and arms of the most wilful, to terrify the rest, for they believe if they lose a member, they cannot return home again: I was advis'd by some of my officers to do the same, but I could not be perswaded to entertain the least thought of it, much less put in practice such barbarity and cruelty to poor creatures, who, excepting their want of Christianity and true religion (their misfortune more than fault) are as much the works of God's hands, and no doubt as dear to him as ourselves; nor can I imagine why they should be despis'd for their colour, being what they cannot help, and the effect of the climate it has pleas'd God to appoint them. I can't think there is any intrinsick value in one colour more than another, nor that white is better than black, only we think so because we are so, and are prone to judge favourably in our own case, as well as the blacks, who in odium of the colour, say, the devil is white, and so paint him. . . .

When our slaves are aboard we shackle the men two and two, while we lie in port, and in sight of their own country, for 'tis then they attempt to make their escape, and mutiny; to prevent which we always keep centinels upon the hatchways, and have a chest full of small arms, ready loaden and prim'd, constantly lying at hand upon the quarterdeck, together with some granada shells; and two of our quarterdeck guns, pointing on the deck thence, and two more out of the steerage, the door of which is always kept shut, and well barr'd; they are fed twice a day, at 10 in the morning, and 4 in the evening, which is the time they are aptest to mutiny, being all upon deck; therefore all that time, what of our men are not employ'd in distributing their victuals to them, and settling them, stand to their arms; and some with lighted matches at the great guns that yaun upon them, loaden with partridge, till they have done and gone down to their kennels between decks. . . .

When we come to sea we let them all out of irons, they never attempting then to rebel, considering that should they kill or master us, they could not tell how to manage the ship, or must trust us, who would carry them where we pleas'd; therefore the only danger is while we are in sight of their own country, which they are lo[a]th to part with; but once out of sight out of mind: I never heard that they mutiny'd in any ships of consequence, that had a good number of men, and the least care; but in small tools [vessels] where they had but few men, and those negligent or drunk, then they surpriz'd and butcher'd them, cut the cables, and let the vessel drive ashore, and every one shift for himself. However, we have some 30 or 40 gold coast negroes, which we buy, and are procur'd us there by our factors, to make guardians and overseers of the Whidaw negroes, and sleep among them to keep them from quarrelling; and in order, as well as to give us notice, if they can discover any caballing or plotting among them, which trust they will discharge with great diligence: they also take care to make the negroes scrape the decks where they lodge every morning very clean, to eschew any distempers that may engender from filth and nastiness; when we constitute a guardian, we give him a cat of nine tails [whip] as a badge of his office, which he is not a little proud of, and will exercise with great authority. We often at sea in the evenings would let the slaves come up into the sun to air themselves, and make them jump and dance for an hour or two to our bagpipes, harp, and fiddle, by which exercise to preserve them in health; but notwithstanding all our endeavour, 'twas my hard fortune to have great sickness and mortality among them.

Having bought my compliment of 700 slaves, viz. 480 men and 220 women, and finish'd all my business at Whidaw, I took my leave of the old king . . . and parted, with many affection—ate expressions on both sides, being forced to promise him that I would return again the next year, with several things he desired me to bring him from England. . . .

Malachy Postelthwayt, *The National and Private Advantages of the African Trade Considered,* 1746

The most approved Judges of the commercial Interests of these Kingdoms have ever been of Opinion, that our West-India and Africa Trades are the most nationally beneficial of any we carry on. It is also allowed on all Hands, that the Trade to Africa is the Branch which renders our American Colonies and Plantations so advantagious [sic] to Great-Britain; that Traffic only affording our Planters a constant Supply of Negroes . . . for the Culture of their Lands in the Produce of Sugars, Tobacco, Rice, Rum . . . Fustick, Pimento, and all other our Plantations Produce: So that the extensive Employment of our Shipping in, to, and from America, the great Brood of Seamen consequent thereupon, and the daily Bread of the most considerable Part of our British Manufacturers, are owing primarily to the Labour of Negroes; who, as they were the first happy Instruments of raising our Plantations; so their Labour only can support and preserve them, and render them still more and more profitable to their Mother-Kingdom. The Negroe Trade therefore, and the natural Consequences resulting from it, may be justly esteemed an inexhaustible Fund of Wealth and Naval Power to this Nation.

D. A Letter from Peter Fontaine, Virginia planter, 1757:

As to your second query, if enslaving our fellow creatures be a practice agreeable to Christianity, it is answered in a great measure in many treatises at home, to which I refer you. I shall only mention something of our present state here.

Like Adam we are all apt to shift off the blame from ourselves and lay it upon others, how justly in our case you may judge. The Negroes are enslaved by the Negroes themselves before they are purchased by the masters of the ships who bring them here. It is to be sure at our choice whether we buy them or not, so this then is our crime, folly, or whatever you will please to call it. But, our Assembly, foreseeing the ill consequences of importing such numbers amongst us, hath often attempted to lay a duty upon them which would amount to a prohibition, such as ten or twenty pounds a head, but no governor dare pass such a law, having instructions to the contrary from the Board of Trade at home. By this means they are forced upon us, whether we will or will not. This plainly shows the African Company hath the advantage of the colonies, and may do as it pleases with the ministry. . . . But to live in Virginia without slaves is morally impossible. Before our troubles, you could not hire a servant or slave for love or money, so that unless robust enough to cut wood, to go to mill, to work at the hoe, etc., you must starve, or board in some family where they both fleece and half starve you. There is no set price upon corn, wheat and provisions, so they take advantage of the necessities of strangers, who are thus obliged to purchase some slaves and land. . . . A common labourer, white or black, if you can be so much favoured as to hire one, is a shilling sterling or fifteen pence currency per day; a bungling carpenter two shillings or two shillings and sixpence per day; besides diet and lodging. That is, for a lazy fellow to get wood and water, £19. 16. 3, current per annum; add to this seven or eight pounds more and you have a slave for life.

Sources: "Letters from the Kings of the Kongo to the King of Portugal," *Monumenta Missionaria Africana*, ed. Antonio Brasio (Lisboa: Agencia Geral do Ultramar, 1952), 1:262–63, 294–95, 335, 404, 470, 488, trans. Linda Wimmer; *Sources of the Western Tradition*, 4th ed., ed. Marvin Perry, Joseph R. Peden and Theodore H. Von Laue (Boston: Houghton Mifflin); Malachy Postelthwayt, *The National and Private Advantages of the African Trade Considered* (London: John and Paul Knapton, 1746); and Ann Maury, ed., *Memoirs of a Huguenot Family* (New York: G. P. Putnam and Company, 1853), 351–52.

REVIEW QUESTIONS

Why does Mvemba a Nzinga protest the Portuguese slave trade? Does he seem to object to the practice of slavery in general or to specific aspects of the trade as carried out by the Portuguese?

How does the seventeenth-century slave trader feel about his slaves? Why? Does racism color his account?

How do Malachy Postelthwayt and Peter Fontaine justify slavery and the slave trade?

Document 57

Canassatego, Onandaga Chief and Spokesman for the Iroquois Nation, *Address to the Europeans*, 1742

This address to Europeans is from Canassatego, an Onandaga chief and spokesman for the Iroquois nation, at a treaty conference in Philadelphia in 1742 as recorded by Benjamin Franklin. In the 1730s officials of the Pennsylvania colony agreed to recognize the Iroquois as the owner of all Indian lands in Pennsylvania, while the Iroquois agreed in turn to sell lands only to Pennsylvania representatives. By the 1740s Canassatego attempted to set terms for future transactions.

We know our lands are now become more valuable: the white people think we do not know their value; but we are sensible that the land is everlasting, and the few goods we receive for it are soon worn out and gone. For the future we will sell no lands but when Brother Onas [the proprietor of Pennsylvania] is in the country; and we will know beforehand the quantity of the goods we are to receive. Besides, we are not well used with respect to the lands still unsold by us. Your people daily settle on these lands, and spoil our hunting. . . . If you have not done anything, we now renew our request, and desire you will inform the person whose people are seated on our lands, that that country belongs to us, in right of conquest; we having bought it with our blood, and taken it from our enemies in fair war. . . . It is customary with us to make a present of skins whenever we renew our treaties. We are ashamed to offer our brethren so few; but your horses and cows have eat the grass our deer used to feed on. This has made them scarce, and will, we hope, plead in excuse for our not bringing a larger quantity: if we could have spared more we would have given more; but we are really poor; and desire you'll not consider the quantity, but, few as they are, accept them in testimony of our regard. . . . Our wise forefathers established union and amity between the Five Nations. This has made us formidable. This has given us great weight and authority with our neighboring nations. We are a powerful Confederacy, and by your observing the same methods our wise forefathers have taken you will acquire fresh strength and power; therefore, whatever befalls you, do not fall out with one another.

Source: Carl Van Doren and Julian P. Boyd, eds., *Indian Treaties Printed by Benjamin Franklin 1736–1762* (Philadelphia: Historical Society of Pennsylvania, 1938), 75.

REVIEW QUESTIONS

Why is Canassatego concerned about Pennsylvanian westward expansion?

What remedy does he suggest?

Do the Indians that Canassatego represents appear to you as passive victims of European expansion?

Document 58

Anonymous, The Declaration of the Rights of Man and of the Citizen, 1789

The following document, approved by the National Assembly in France on August 26, 1789, and attached to the French Constitution of 1791, echoed the Enlightenment ideas that were then prevalent in the Atlantic World. During the eighteenth century, European political philosophers such as Voltaire and Jean-Jacques Rousseau employed arguments based on reason to attack dogma that buttressed the position of the church and the state. The French proclamation, following in the footsteps of the American Declaration of Independence, asserted that individuals have certain natural and inalienable rights. The deputies in the National Assembly regarded their declaration as a preliminary step to the establishment of a Constitutional monarchy. In a pamphlet written in September 1791, Olympe de Gouges, a vocal feminist in Revolutionary France, argued that women are endowed with the same natural rights as men and that they should receive equal treatment before the law. The National Assembly ignored her appeal, even though the deputies had voted in May 1791 to grant full citizenship to nonwhite males born to free parents in all French colonies. Nevertheless, de Gouges remained an active proponent for the principle of gender equality until November 1793 when she was executed for criticizing the newly established regime headed by Maximilien Robespierre.

The representatives of the people of France, formed into a National Assembly, considering that ignorance, neglect, or contempt of the rights, are the sole causes of public misfortunes and corruptions of Government, have resolved to set forth in a solemn declaration, these natural, imprescriptible, and inalienable rights; that this declaration being constantly present to the minds of the members of the body social, they may be ever kept attentive to their rights and duties; that the acts of the legislative and executive powers of Government, being capable of being every moment compared with the end of political institutions, may be more respected; and also, that the future claims of the citizens, being directed by simple and incontestable principles, may always tend to the maintenance of the Constitution, and the general happiness.

For these reasons the National Assembly doth recognize and declare, in the presence of the Supreme Being, and with the hope of his blessing and favour, the following *sacred* rights of men and of citizens:

Men are born, and always continue, free and equal in respect of their rights. Civil distinctions, therefore, can be founded only on public utility.

The end of all political associations is the preservation of the natural and imprescriptible rights of man; and these rights are Liberty, Property, Security, and Resistance of Oppression.

The Nation is essentially the source of all sovereignty; nor can any individual, or any body of men, be entitled to any authority which is not expressly derived from it.

Political Liberty consists in the power of doing whatever does not injure another. The exercise of the natural rights of every man has no other limits than those which are necessary to secure to every *other* man the free exercise of the same rights; and these limits are determinable only by the law.

The law ought to prohibit only actions hurtful to society. What is not prohibited by the law should not be hindered; nor should anyone be compelled to that which the law does not require.

The law is an expression of the will of the community. All citizens have a right to concur, either personally or by their representatives, in its formation. It should be the same to all, whether it protects or punishes; and all being equal in its sight, are equally eligible to all honours, places, and employments, according to their different abilities, without any other distinction than that created by their virtues and talents.

No man should be accused, arrested, or held in confinement, except in cases determined by the law, and according to the forms which it has prescribed. All who promote, solicit, transmitting, execute, or cause to be executed, arbitrary orders, ought to be punished, and every citizen called upon or apprehended by virtue of the law ought immediately to obey, and renders himself culpable by resistance.

The law ought to impose no other penalties but such as are absolutely and evidently necessary; and no one ought to be punished, but in virtue of a law promulgated before the offence, and legally applied.

Every man being presumed innocent till he has been convicted, whenever his detention becomes indispensable, all rigor to him, more than necessary to secure his person, ought to be provided against by the law.

No man ought to be molested on account of his opinions, not even on account of his religious opinions, provided his avowal of them does not disturb the public order established by the law.

The unrestrained communication of thoughts and opinions being one of the most precious of the Rights of Man, every citizen may speak, write, and publish freely, provided he is responsible for the abuse of this liberty, in cases determined by the law.

A public force being necessary to give security to the Rights of Men and of citizens, that force is instituted for the benefit of the community and not for the particular benefit of the persons with whom it is intrusted.

A common contribution being necessary for the support of the public force, and for defraying the other expenses of Government, it ought to be divided equally among the members of the community, according to their abilities.

Every citizen has a right, either by himself or his representative, to a free voice in determining the necessity of public contributions, the appropriation of them, and their amount, mode of assessment, and duration.

Every community has a right to demand of all its agents an account of their conduct.

Every community in which a separation of powers and a security of rights is not provided for, wants a Constitution.

The right to property being inviolable and sacred, no one ought to be deprived of it, except in cases of evident public necessity, legally ascertained, and on condition of a previous just indemnity.

Source: Thomas Paine, *Rights of Man: Being an Answer to Mr. Burke's Attack on the French Revolution* (London: J. M. Dent & Sons, Ltd., 1915), 94–97.

REVIEW QUESTIONS

What were the rights that the National Assembly deemed natural?

What did the National Assembly mean by political liberty?

How did the National Assembly view the role of laws?

Document 59

William Wilberforce, On the Horrors of the Slave Trade, 1789

The Enlightenment beliefs that all men are created equal and endowed with the same basic rights presented a fundamental challenge to the institution of slavery. Great Britain took the lead in pushing for the abolition of the slave trade and for the elimination of slavery in the Atlantic World. As an evangelical Christian, William Wilberforce played a prominent role in the British antislavery movement. Wilberforce became a member of the House of Commons in 1780, and he soon began advocating antislavery legislation. On May 12, 1789, he delivered a speech in Parliament, excerpted here, in support of his own resolution condemning the slave trade. Parliament responded to growing abolitionist sentiment in England in 1807 by passing a law that prohibited British merchants from participating in the slave trade. During the next decade, the US, France, and the Netherlands also made it illegal for their merchants to buy and sell slaves. Wilberforce subsequently began fighting to eliminate slavery in British overseas possessions, and a month after he died in 1833, the House of Lords passed a law abolishing slavery in most of the British Empire.

What should we suppose must naturally be the consequence of our carrying on a slave trade with Africa? With a country vast in its extent, not utterly barbarous, but civilized in a very small degree? Does any one suppose a slave trade would help their civilization? Is it not plain that Africa must suffer from it, that civilization must be checked, that her barbarous manners must be made more barbarous, and that the happiness of her millions of inhabitants must be prejudiced by her contact with Britain? Does not everyone see that a slave trade carried on around African coasts must carry violence and desolation to its very center? . . .

I must now speak of the transit of the slaves to the West Indies. This, I confess, in my own opinion, is the most wretched part of the whole subject. So much misery condensed in so little room is more than the human imagination had ever before conceived. . . .

Let any one imagine to himself six or seven hundred of these wretches chained two and two, surrounded with every object that is nauseous and disgusting, diseased, and struggling under every kind of wretchedness! How can we bear to think of such a scene as this? . . .

In order, however, not to trust too much to any sort of description, I will call the attention of the House to one kind of evidence, which is absolutely infallible. Death, at least, is a sure ground of evidence, and the proportion of deaths will not only confirm, but, if possible, will even aggravate our suspicion of their misery in the transit. It will be found, upon an average of all ships of which evidence has been given at the privy council, that exclusive of those who perish before they sail, not less than twelve and one-half per cent perish in the passage. Besides these, the Jamaica report tells you that not less than four and one-half per cent die on shore before the day of sale, which is only a week or two from the time of landing. One-third more die in the climate, and this in a country exactly like their own, where they are healthy and happy, as some of the evidence would pretend. The diseases, however, which they contract on shipboard, the astringent washes that hide their wounds, and the deceitful tricks used to make them up for sale, are, as the Jamaica report indicates, one principal cause of this mortality. Upon the whole, however, here is a mortality of about fifty per cent, and this among Negroes who are not bought unless quite healthy at first, and unless (as the phrase is with cattle) they are sound in wind and limb. . . .

What mortification must we feel at having so long neglected to think about our guilt, or to attempt any reparation! . . .

Let us put an end at once to this inhuman traffic—let us stop this effusion of human blood. . . .

And, sir, when we think of eternity, and of the future consequences of all human conduct, what is there in this life that should make any man contradict the dictates of his conscience, the principles of justice, the laws of religion, and of God? Sir, the nature and all the circumstances of this trade are now laid open to us; we can no longer plead ignorance, we cannot evade it; it is now an object placed before us, we cannot pass it; we may spurn it, we may kick it out of our way, but we cannot turn aside so as to avoid seeing it; for it is brought now so directly before our eyes that this House must decide, and must justify to all the world, and to their own consciences, the rectitude of the grounds and principles of their decision.

Source: William Jennings Bryan, ed., *The World's Famous Orations* (New York: Funk and Wagnalls, 1906), 4:60–70.

REVIEW QUESTIONS

What aspect of the slave trade does Wilberforce view as causing the greatest suffering?

What does he view as the most damning evidence for the evils of the slave trade?

How does he attempt to persuade Parliament to abolish the slave trade?

Document 60

George Washington, Farewell Address, 1796

Before completing his second term as president of the US, George Washington delivered his famous valedictory to the American people. His address, published in the *American Daily Advertiser* on September 17, 1796, provided guidelines that influenced the future diplomacy of the US. Although some Americans favored pro-British policies and others advocated pro-French policies, Washington argued that the US should base its foreign policies on national interest rather than any emotional attachments. And he believed that if the young US adopted a policy of neutrality, the time was not far off when it could choose peace or war as its interests dictated. His injunctions, contained in the following excerpts from the address, were designed to assure the success of the new nation, composed of thirteen former British colonies, on what he and his colleagues often referred to as "our rising American Empire."

Observe good faith and justice toward all nations. Cultivate peace and harmony with all. . . .

In the execution of such a plan nothing is more essential than that permanent, inveterate antipathies against particular nations and passionate attachments for others should be excluded, and that in place of them just and amicable feelings toward all should be cultivated. The nation which indulges toward another an habitual hatred or an habitual fondness is in some degree a slave. It is a slave to its animosity or to its affection, either of which is sufficient to lead it astray from its duty and its interest. Antipathy in one nation against another disposes each more readily to offer insult and injury, to lay hold of slight causes of umbrage, and to be haughty and intractable when accidental or trifling occasions of dispute occur. . . .

So, likewise, a passionate attachment of one nation for another produces a variety of evils. Sympathy for the favorite nation, facilitating the illusion of an imaginary common interest in cases where no real common interest exists, and the infusing into one the enmities of the other, betrays the former into a participation in the quarrels and wars of the latter without adequate inducement or justification. It leads also to concessions to the favorite nation of privileges denied to others, which is apt doubly to injure the nation making the concessions by unnecessarily parting with what ought to have been retained, and by exciting ill will, and a disposition to retaliate in the parties from whom equal privileges are withheld; and it gives to ambitious, corrupted, or deluded citizens (who devote themselves to the favorite nation) facility to betray or sacrifice the interests of their own country without odium, or a laudable zeal for public good the base or foolish compliances of ambition, corruption, or infatuation. . . .

Against the insidious wiles of foreign influence (I conjure you to believe me, fellow citizens) the jealousy of a free people ought to be *constantly* awake, since history and experience prove that foreign influence is one of the most baneful foes of republican government. But that jealousy, to be useful, must be impartial, else it becomes the instrument of the very influence to be avoided, instead of a defense against it. Excessive partiality for one foreign nation and excessive dislike of another cause those whom they actuate to see danger only on one side, and serve to veil and even second the arts of influence on the other. Real patriots who may resist the intrigues of the favorite are liable to become suspected and odious, while its tools and dupes usurp the applause and confidence of the people to surrender their interests.

The great rule of conduct for us in regard to foreign nations is, in extending our commercial relations to have with them as little *political* connection as possible. So far as we have already formed engagements let them be fulfilled with perfect good faith. Here let us stop.

Europe has a set of primary interests which to us have none or a very remote relation. Hence she must be engaged in frequent controversies, the causes of which are essentially foreign to our concerns. Hence, therefore, it must be unwise in us to implicate ourselves by artificial ties in the ordinary vicissitudes of her polities or the ordinary combinations and collusions of her friendships or enmities.

Our detached and distant situation invites and enables us to pursue a different course. If we remain one people, under an efficient government, the period is not far off when we may take such an attitude as will cause the neutrality we may at any time resolve upon to be scrupulously respected; when belligerent nations, under the impossibility of making acquisitions upon us, will not lightly hazard the giving us provocation; when we may choose peace or war, as our interest, guided by justice, shall counsel. . . .

It is our true policy to steer clear of permanent alliances with any portion of the foreign world, so far, I mean, as we are now at liberty to do it; for let me not be understood as capable of patronizing infidelity to existing engagements. I hold the maxim no less applicable to public than to private affairs that honesty is always the best policy. I repeat, therefore, let those engagements be observed in their genuine sense. But in my opinion it is unnecessary as it would be unwise to extend them.

Taking care always to keep ourselves by suitable establishments on a respectable defensive posture, we may safely trust to temporary alliances for extraordinary emergencies.

Harmony, liberal intercourse with all nations are recommended by policy, humanity, and interest. But even our commercial policy should hold an equal and impartial hand, neither seeking nor granting exclusive favors or preferences; consulting the natural course of things; diffusing and diversifying by gentle means the streams of commerce, but forcing nothing; establishing with powers so disposed, in order to give trade a stable course, to define the rights of our merchants, and to enable the Government to support them, conventional rules of intercourse, the best that present circumstances and mutual opinion will permit, but temporary and liable to be from time to time abandoned or varied as experience and circumstances shall dictate; constantly keeping in view that it is folly in one nation to look for disinterested favors from another; that it must pay with a portion of its independence for whatever it may accept under that character; that by such acceptance it may place itself in the condition of having given equivalents for nominal favors, and yet being reproached with ingratitude for not giving more. There can be no greater error than to expect or calculate upon real favors from one nation to another. It is an illusion which experience must cure. . . .

Source: James D. Richardson, ed., *Messages and Papers of the Presidents* (New York: Bureau of National Literature, Inc., 1897), I:205–16.

REVIEW QUESTIONS

Why does Washington argue that the US should avoid holding either strong antipathies or passionate attachments to foreign nations?

What policies does he advise the US to pursue regarding commercial and political relations with foreign countries?

Would you describe Washington as an idealist or a realist?

Document 61

Thomas R. Malthus, An Essay on the Principle of Population, 1798

In 1798, Thomas R. Malthus, a prominent scholar of political economy, published his famous essay on population. Malthus asserted that throughout history increases in the food supply led families to have more children, thereby bringing living standards back to subsistence levels. And he argued that the scourges of famine, plague, and war had repeatedly curbed demographic growth. As indicated by the excerpts of his essay reprinted here, Malthus believed that what we now call per capita gross domestic product (GDP) could not continue to grow in England or any other country because population would increase at a faster pace than the means of subsistence. The Industrial Revolution, however, enabled Britain to escape the Malthusian trap. Between 1750 and 1850, the English population rapidly increased from around 6 million to about 16 million, primarily because women married at a younger age and had more children than in the past. Yet, at the same time, production increased at a faster rate than births, thereby allowing England to become the first country in the history of the world to enjoy a sustained growth in per capita income while experiencing a massive expansion in population. Moreover, beginning around 1890, a handful of advanced industrial nations experienced a demographic transition or a shift from the traditional pattern of high birth and death rates to a new pattern of low fertility and mortality. In these countries, as women began having fewer children, population growth slowed, and per capita income rose to higher and higher levels.

I have read some of the speculations on the perfectibility of man and of society with great pleasure. I have been warmed and delighted with the enchanting picture which they hold forth. I ardently wish for such happy improvements. But I see great, and, to my understanding, unconquerable difficulties in the way of them. These difficulties it is my present purpose to state, declaring, at the same time, that so far from exulting in them, as a cause of triumph over the friends of innovation, nothing would give me greater pleasure than to see them completely removed. . . .

I think I may fairly make two postulata.

First, That food is necessary to the existence of man.

Secondly, That the passion between the sexes is necessary and will remain nearly in its present state.

These two laws, ever since we have had any knowledge of mankind, appear to have been fixed laws of our nature, and, as we have not hitherto seen any alteration in them, we have no right to conclude that they will ever cease to be what they are now, without an immediate act of power in that Being who first arranged the system of the universe, and for the advantage of his creatures, still executes, according to fixed laws, all its various operations. . . .

Assuming then, my postulata as granted, I say, that the power of population is indefinitely greater than the power in the earth to produce subsistence for man.

Population, when unchecked, increases in a geometrical ratio. Subsistence increases only in an arithmetical ratio. A slight acquaintance with numbers will shew the immensity of the first power in comparison of the second.

By that law of our nature which makes food necessary to the life of man, the effects of these two unequal powers must be kept equal.

This implies a strong and constantly operating check on population from the difficulty of subsistence. This difficulty must fall some where and must necessarily be severely felt by a large portion of mankind. . . .

The way in which these effects are produced seems to be this. We will suppose the means of subsistence in any country just equal to the ease of support of its inhabitants. The constant effort towards population, which is found to act even in the most vicious societies, increases the number of people before the means of subsistence are increased. The food therefore which before supported seven millions must now be divided among seven millions and a half or eight millions. The poor consequently must live much worse, and many of them be reduced to severe distress. The number of labourers also being above the proportion of work in the market, the price of labour must tend toward a decrease, while the price of provisions would at the same time tend to rise. The labourer therefore must work harder to earn the same as he did before. During this season of distress, the discouragements to marriage and the difficulty of rearing a family are so great that population is at a stand. In the mean time the cheapness of labour, the plenty of labourers, and the necessity of an increase in industry amongst them, encourages cultivators to employ more labour upon their land, to turn up fresh soil, and to manure and improve more completely what is already in tillage, till ultimately the means of subsistence become in the same proportion to the population as at the period from which we set out. The situation of the labourer being then again tolerably comfortable, the restraints to population are in some degree loosened, and the same retrograde and progressive movements with respect to happiness are repeated.

This sort of oscillation will not be remarked by superficial observers, and it may be difficult even for the most penetrating mind to calculate its periods. Yet that in all old states some such vibration does exist, though from various transverse causes, in a much less marked, and in a much more irregular manner than I have described it, no reflecting man who considers the subject deeply can well doubt. . . .

That population cannot increase without the means of subsistence is a proposition so evident that it needs no illustration.

That population does invariably increase where there are the means of subsistence, the history of every people that have ever existed will abundantly prove.

And that the superior power of population cannot be checked without producing misery or vice, the ample portion of these two bitter ingredients in the cup of human life and the continuance of the physical causes that seem to have produced them bear too convincing a testimony. . . .

Source: Thomas Malthus, *An Essay on the Principle of Population* (London: Printed for J. Johnson, in St. Paul's Church-Yard, 1798), 3–10.

REVIEW QUESTIONS

What assumptions does Malthus make concerning the human condition?

What kind of production does he view as the economic basis of societies?

Why does he believe societies vacillate between being comfortable and miserable?

Document 62

Michael Sadler,
A Parliamentary Committee Report on
Child Labor in England, 1832

The Industrial Revolution, while spurring a basic shift in the distribution of the population from rural areas to urban centers, had a profound impact on living conditions in England. Unlike farmers, factory operatives had to work during fixed hours while machines were running. They could not choose when to start or stop work or when to perform different tasks during the day. Moreover, British industrial workers often found themselves living in unhealthy conditions in densely populated urban slums. Frequently suffering from dysentery and tuberculosis caused by contaminated water or polluted air, urban dwellers usually died at an earlier age than their rural counterparts. Textile manufacturing stood at the forefront of the British Industrial Revolution. By 1830, a half million out of 12 million people living in England were employed in cotton factories. Many were unskilled women and children who worked long hours for low wages and often suffered from poor health owing to breathing air filled with fibers. In 1832, Michael Sadler chaired a parliamentary committee that conducted an investigation into the conditions of labor in British textile factories. The following selection provides a typical example of the testimony given by many children to the committee.

William Cooper, called in; and Examined

What is your business?—I follow the cloth-dressing at present.
What is your age?—I was eight and twenty last February.
When did you first begin to work in mills or factories?—When I was about 10 years of age.
With whom did you first work?—At Mr. Benyon's flax mills in Meadowland, Leeds.

What were your usual hours of working?—We began at five, and gave over at nine; at five o'clock in the morning.

And you gave over at nine o'clock?—At nine at night.

At what distance might you have lived from the mill?—About a mile and a half.

At what time had you to get up in the morning to attend your labour?—I had to be up soon after four o'clock.

Every morning?—Every morning.

What intermissions had you for meals?—When we began at five in the morning, we went on until noon, and then we had forty minutes for dinner.

Had you no time for breakfast?—No, we got as we could, while we were working.

Had you any time for an afternoon refreshment, or what is called in Yorkshire your "drinking?"—No, when we began at noon, we went till night; there was only one stoppage, the 40 minutes for dinner.

Then as you had to get your breakfast, and what is called "drinking" in that manner, you had to put it on one side?—Yes, we had to put it on one side; and when we got our frames doffed, we ate two or three mouthfuls, and then put it by again.

Is there not considerable dust in a flax mill?—A flax mill is very dusty indeed.

Was not your food therefore frequently spoiled?—Yes, at times with the dust; sometimes we could not eat it, when it had got a lot of dust on.

What were you when you were ten years old?—What is called a bobbin-doffer; when the frames are quite full we have to doff them.

Then as you lived so far from home, you took your dinner to the mill?—We took all our meals with us, living so far off.

During the 40 minutes which you were allowed for dinner, had you ever to employ that time in your turn cleaning the machinery?—At times we had to stop to clean the machinery, and then we got our dinner as well as we could; they paid us for that.

At times you had no resting as all?—No.

How much had you for cleaning the machinery?—I cannot exactly say what they gave us, as I never took any notice of it.

Did you ever work even later than the time you have mentioned?—I cannot say that I worked later there: I had a sister who worked up stairs, and she worked till 11 at night, in what they call the card-room.

At what time in the morning did she begin to work?—At the same time as myself.

And they kept her there till 11 at night?—Till 11 at night.

You say that your sister was in the card-room?—Yes.

Is that not a very dusty department?—Yes, very dusty indeed.

She had to be at the mill at five, and was kept at work till eleven at night?—Yes.

During the whole time she was there?—During the whole time; there was only 40 minutes allowed at dinner out of that.

To keep you at work for such a length of time, and especially towards the termination of such a day's labour as that, what means were taken to keep you awake and attentive?—They strapped us at times, when we were not quite ready to be doffing the frame when it was full.

Were you frequently strapped?—At times we were frequently strapped.

What sort of strap was it?—About this length.

What was it made of?—Of leather.

Were you occasionally very considerably hurt with the strap?—Sometimes it hurt us very much, and sometimes they did not lay on so hard as they did at others.

Were the girls strapped in that sort of way?—They did not strap what they called the grown-up women.

Were any of the female children strapped?—Yes; they were strapped in the same way as the lesser boys.

How long did you work in that mill?—Five years.

And how did it agree with [y]our health?—I was sometimes well, and sometimes not very well.

Did it affect your breathing at all?—Yes; sometimes I was stuffed. . . .

After working at the mill [a different one] in this excess, how did you fine your health at last?—I found it very bad indeed; I found illness coming on me a long time before I fell down.

Did you at length become so ill as to be unable to pursue your work?—I was obliged to give it up entirely.

How long were you ill?—For six months.

Who attended? Mr. Metcalf and Mr. Freeman.

What were you told by your medical attendants was the reason of your illness?—Nothing but hard work, and working long hours; and they gave me up, and said no good could be done for me, that I must go into the country.

Did this excessive labour not only weaken you, but destroy your appetite?—It destroyed the appetite, and I became so feeble, that I could not cross the floor unless I had a stick to go with; I was in great pain, and I could find ease in no posture.

You could drink in the meantime, if you could not eat?—Yes, I could drink.

But you found that did not improve your health?—No.

Has it been remarked that your excessive labour from early life has greatly diminished your growth?—A number of persons have said that such was the case, and that I was the same as if I had been made of iron or stone.

What height are you?—About five feet. It is that that has hindered me of my growth.

When you were somewhat recovered, did you apply for labour?—I applied for my work again, but the overlooker said I was not fit to work; he was sure of that, and he would not let me have it. I was obliged to throw myself on the parish [for poor relief].

Have you subsisted on the parish ever since?—Yes.

Have you been always willing to work?—I was always willing and anxious to work from my infancy. . . .

Source: *British Parliamentary Papers: Reports from Committees* (London: House of Commons, 1832), 15:6–9.

REVIEW QUESTIONS

According to the testimony, how many hours a day did the textile operative work?

How old was he when he was first employed in a textile factory?

How did his factory jobs affect his health?

Document 63

Lin Zexu, The Chinese Reaction to British Opium Traders, 1839

In 1839, the Chinese emperor dispatched Lin Zexu to Canton to stop British merchants from shipping opium to China. Before taking direct action against the British opium traders, Lin sent a warning to Queen Victoria. When he did not receive any reply to his latter, excerpted here, Lin confiscated more than two hundred chests of opium from foreign merchants operating in Canton and dumped the drugs into the sea. The British government used the incident as an excuse to go to war with China in hopes of prying open a huge market, especially for Manchester cotton manufacturers who dreamed of selling their products to several hundred million Chinese consumers. In 1842, the first Opium War ended with the Treaty of Nanjing, which gave British merchants the freedom to trade with anyone in Canton and four additional Chinese ports. The treaty also granted British residents in these ports immunity from Chinese laws and fixed Chinese tariffs at low rates.

We find that your country is distant from us . . . that your foreign ships come hither striving the one with the other for our trade, and for the simple reason of their strong desire to reap a profit. . . . By what principle of reason then, should these foreigners send in return a poisonous drug, which involves in destruction those very natives of China? Without meaning to say that the foreigners harbor such destructive intentions in their hearts, we yet positively assert that from their inordinate thirst after gain, they are perfectly careless about the injuries they inflict upon us! And such being the case, we should like to ask what has become of that conscience which heaven has implanted in the hearts of all men?

We have heard that in your own country opium is prohibited with the utmost strictness and severity:—this is a strong proof that you know full well how hurtful it is to mankind. Since then you do not permit it to injure your own country, you ought not to have the injurious drug transferred to another country, and above all others, how much less to the Inner Land! Of the products which China exports to your foreign countries, there is not one which is not beneficial to mankind in some shape or other. There are those which serve for food, those which are useful, and those which are calculated for re-sale; —but all are beneficial. . . .

Your honorable nation takes away the products of our central land, and not only do you thereby obtain food and support for yourselves, but moreover, by reselling these products to other countries you reap a threefold profit. Now if you would only not sell opium, this threefold profit would be secured to you: how can you possibly consent to forego it for a drug that is hurtful to men, and an unbridled craving after that gain that seems to know no bounds! Let us suppose that foreigners came from another country, and brought opium into England, and seduced the people of your country to smoke it, would not you, the sovereign of the said country, look upon such a procedure with anger, and in your just indignation endeavor to get rid of it? Now we have always heard that your highness possesses a most kind and benevolent heart, surely then you are incapable of doing or causing to be done unto another, that which you should not wish another to do unto you! . . .

Suppose the subject of another country were to come to England to trade, he would certainly be required to comply with the laws of England to trade, then how much more does this apply to us of the celestial empire! Now it is a fixed statute of this empire, that any native Chinese who sells opium is punishable with death and even he who merely smokes it, must not less die. Pause and reflect for a moment: If you foreigners did not bring the opium hither, where should our Chinese people get it to re-sell? It is you foreigners who involve our simple natives in the pit of Death, and are they alone to be permitted to escape alive? If so much as one of those deprive one of our people of his life, he must forfeit his life in requital for that which he has taken:—how much more does this apply to him who by means of opium destroys his fellow-men? Does the havoc which he commits stop with a single life? Therefore it is that those foreigners who import opium into the Central Land are condemned to be beheaded and strangled by the new statute. . . .

Our celestial empire rules over ten thousand kingdoms! Most surely do we possess a measure of godlike majesty which ye cannot fathom! Still we cannot bear to slay or exterminate without previous warning, and it is for this reason that we now clearly make known to you the fixed laws of our land. If the foreign merchants of your said honorable nation desire to continue their commercial intercourse, they must tremblingly obey our recorded statutes, they must cut off for ever the source from which the opium flows. . . .

Let your highness immediately, upon the receipt of this communication, inform us promptly of the state of matters, and of the measure you are pursuing utterly to put a stop to the opium evil. Please let your reply be speedy. Do not on any account make excuses or procrastinate.

Source: *The Chinese Repository*, Vol. VIII, No. 10 (February 1840), 497–503.

REVIEW QUESTIONS

What did Lin believe motivated foreign merchants to ship opium to China?

What kind of appeal did he make in his letter to the British queen?

What did he warn would happen to foreigners who continued to import opium into China?

Elizabeth Cady Stanton, A Demand for Equality for Women, 1848

The Declaration of Sentiments, drafted by Elizabeth Cady Stanton, was signed by sixty-eight women and thirty-two men at a women's rights convention held in July 1848 at Seneca Falls in upstate New York. Despite some opposition, the convention approved a resolution, introduced by Stanton, insisting that women must have the right to vote. The Seneca Falls Convention is regarded by many as the birthplace of American feminism. A series of women's rights conventions were held in the following decades, and in 1920, the female suffrage movement in the US culminated in the passage of the Nineteenth Amendment, which granted women the right to vote. The Declaration of Sentiments is reprinted here.

When, in the course of human events, it becomes necessary for one portion of the family of man to assume among the people of the earth a position different from that which they have hitherto occupied, but one to which the laws of nature and of nature's God entitle them, a decent respect to the opinions of mankind requires that they should declare the causes that impel them to such a course.

We hold these truths to be self-evident; that all men and women are created equal; that they are endowed by their Creator with certain inalienable rights; that among these are life, liberty, and the pursuit of happiness; that to secure these rights governments are instituted, deriving their just powers from the consent of the governed. Whenever any form of Government becomes destructive of these ends, it is the right of those who suffer from it to refuse allegiance to it, and to insist upon the institution of a new government, laying its foundation on such principles, and organizing its powers in such form as to them shall seem most likely to effect their safety and happiness. Prudence, indeed, will dictate that governments long established should not be changed for light and transient causes; and accordingly, all experience hath shown that mankind are more disposed to suffer, while evils are sufferable, than to right themselves, by abolishing the forms to which they are accustomed. But when a long train of abuses and usurpations, pursuing invariably the same object, evinces a design to reduce them under absolute despotism, it is their duty to throw off such government, and to provide new guards for their future security. Such has been the patient sufferance of the women under this government, and such is now the necessity which constrains them to demand the equal station to which they are entitled.

The history of mankind is a history of repeated injuries and usurpations on the part of man toward woman, having in direct object the establishment of an absolute tyranny over her. To prove this, let facts be submitted to a candid world.

He has never permitted her to exercise her inalienable right to the elective franchise.

He has compelled her to submit to laws, in the formation of which she had no voice.

He has withheld from her rights which are given to the most ignorant and degraded men—both natives and foreigners.

Having deprived her of this first right of a citizen, the elective franchise, thereby leaving her without representation in the halls of legislation, he has oppressed her on all sides.

He has made her, if married, in the eye of the law, civilly dead.

He has taken from her all right in property, even to the wages she earns.

He has made her, morally, an irresponsible being, as she can commit many crimes, with impunity, provided they be done in the presence of her husband. In the covenant of marriage, she is compelled to promise obedience to her husband, he becoming, to all intents and purposes, her master—the law giving him power to deprive her of her liberty, and to administer chastisement.

He has so framed the laws of divorce, as to what shall be the proper causes of divorce; in case of separation, to whom the guardianship of the children shall be given, as to be wholly regardless of the happiness of women—the law, in all cases, going upon the false supposition of the supremacy of man, and giving all power into his hands.

After depriving her of all rights as a married woman, if single and the owner of property, he has taxed her to support a government which recognizes her only when her property can be made profitable to it.

He has monopolized nearly all the profitable employments, and from those she is permitted to follow, she receives but a scanty remuneration.

He closes against her all the avenues to wealth and distinction, which he considers most honorable to himself. As a teacher of theology, medicine, or law, she is not known.

He has denied her the facilities for obtaining a thorough education—all colleges being closed against her.

He allows her in Church as well as State, but a subordinate position, claiming Apostolic authority for her exclusion from the ministry, and with some exceptions, from any public participation in the affairs of the Church.

He has created a false public sentiment, by giving to the world a different code of morals for men and women, by which moral delinquencies which exclude women from society, are not only tolerated but deemed of little account in man.

He has usurped the prerogative of Jehovah himself, claiming it as his right to assign for her a sphere of action, when that belongs to her conscience and her God.

He has endeavored, in every way that he could to destroy her confidence in her own powers, to lessen her self-respect, and to make her willing to lead a dependent and abject life.

Now, in view of this entire disfranchisement of one-half the people of this country, their social and religious degradation,—in view of the unjust laws above mentioned, and because women do feel themselves aggrieved, oppressed, and fraudulently deprived of their most sacred rights, we insist that they have immediate admission to all the rights and privileges which belong to them as citizens of these United States.

In entering upon the great work before us, we anticipate no small amount of misconception, misrepresentation, and ridicule; but we shall use every instrumentality within our power to effect our object. We shall employ agents, circulate tracts, petition the State and national Legislatures, and endeavor to enlist the pulpit and the press in our behalf. We hope this Convention will be followed by a series of Conventions, embracing every part of the country.

Source: US National Parks Service https://www.nps.gov/wori/learn/history culture/declaration-of-sentiments.htm.

REVIEW QUESTIONS

What did Stanton regard as the source of women's rights?

How did she view the role of women in families?

Why did she insist that women must have the right to vote?

Document 65

Sergei Stepanovich Lanskoi, The Debate over Abolishing Serfdom in Russia, 1859

The defeat of Russia in the Crimean War (1853–1865), which demonstrated its economic and military weakness, convinced the Russian government of the need to abolish the archaic institution of serfdom. Russian leaders realized that serfdom impeded agricultural productivity and industrial development because unfree peasants had little incentive to make improvements on land owned by the gentry and because impoverished serfs could not provide a large market for manufactured goods made in Russia. Moreover, Russian leaders feared a spontaneous peasant uprising if serfs were not emancipated and given plots of their own land to cultivate. But calls for the emancipation of Russian serfs provoked considerable opposition from estate owners. The committees, representing the nobles in different provinces in the Russian Empire, expressed their views on proposals drafted by government officials for the tsar to approve. In August 1859, in a memorandum excerpted here, Minister of the Interior Sergei Stepanovich Lanskoi briefed Tsar Alexander II on the subject. Despite opposition from the landowning gentry, Alexander II decided in 1861 to issue a Manifesto on the Abolition of Serfdom.

All guberniia (provincial) committees on the peasant question (with the exception of only Perm' and Stavropol') have completed and sent in their work. . . .

The first news about a proposed reform elicited instinctive fear among the landowning gentry. They expected outrages at its publication and complete loss of their property when it would be carried out. . . .

In order to pacify their minds and direct their thinking, at Your order, a whole series of measures was undertaken to clarify all subjects that were eliciting doubts. . . .

Little by little the fears began to dissipate; the idea of the possibility and the necessity of this transformation began to gain ground. . . .

The principle of allowing peasants to continue to live where they do currently, so indispensable for securing their way of life, had the positive effect also of pushing the committees to think about offering peasants the opportunity to buy not only their residences, but their plots of land as well.

Generally speaking in the majority of the committees' proposals . . . there was expressed the intent to liberate the peasants without land, and, at the same time make their transition more difficult. The authors of the proposals complain that for lack of capital their land will lack for workers. . . .

Not getting lost in a mass of details, we can derive from a general overview of committee proposals the following prevailing opinions: *The first opinion* is of those who have shown little sympathy for the emancipation of the peasants, driven by the personal material privileges enjoyed by the landowner. . . . The majority of these people were born and brought up in the thoughtways of serfdom and cannot grasp the burning need for change, expecting only certain losses. Their fearful imaginings hold that they and their descendants will be pauperized. . . .

The second opinion. This grew out of that approach focusing on personal material interests. . . . Its adherents are most of all among our pomeshchiki of high rank and wealth. Prioritizing the estate interests of the nobility, they wish to establish in Russia a landed aristocracy similar to that of England, and instead of the current privileged noble property that exists on the basis of serfdom, they wish to introduce a no less privileged one on a feudal basis. In exchange for offering the peasants their residences as private property and the use of fields, they wish to reserve to the landowners . . . rights reminiscent of medieval feudal privileges in the West. . . . [However,] their real goal is emancipation of the peasants without land.

The third opinion is held by those who are in favor of a complete destruction of serfdom. They are, while far from the majority, a significant proportion of the Russian nobility. While in sympathy with the views of the government respecting the need to protect the individual peasant from others' whims and for a solid securing of land to the peasant, they differ among themselves on many specific issues. But their opinions, the fruit of independently coming to their convictions through the difficult path of long study of the question from all angles . . . unanimously favor the total abolition of landowner power and the right of the peasants to an obligatory or discretional buy-out of all or a part of their land currently worked for their own sustenance. . . .

Among those who hold the first two opinions there has recently been observed the desire to bring to life some kind of clear expression of what they call *public opinion*, in order to deflect the government's direction . . . . Serfs have long been excited by the thought of freedom. Already ideas have long circulated among them that the Tsar wants their freedom, but that the nobility is blocking that cause. . . .

Buy-outs of land by peasants through voluntary negotiations could take a lot of time. For that reason, we must immediately give peasants individual rights, and to secure these rights we must enhance the police, open new institutions for the settlement of disputes and misunderstandings between peasants and landowners, allow peasants to keep land currently farmed for themselves, with only some changes; and immediately lessen their obligations, bringing them into line with the amount of land they will have. But in order to compensate the nobles for the loss of landlord power, we must grant them pride of place in local economic administration; and for that, in order to secure for them moral authority over local residents, it would be useful to give them a direct role in elections for justices of the peace and other positions common to both estates, such as noble and peasant assemblies.

Source: "A Look at the Situation of the Peasant Question at the Present Time (August 1859). Russkii arkiv (Russian Archive), 1869, vyp. (issue) 8, 1364–76. [This document has been translated for us by Professor Douglas R. Weiner of the University of Arizona.]

REVIEW QUESTIONS

What did Lanskoi report to be the majority opinion expressed by the gentry?

What did he report to be the minority opinion expressed by the gentry?

How did he advise that that the emancipation of the serfs should be implemented?

Document 66

Boston *Commercial Bulletin,* Indians as Obstacles to the Development of the West, 1867

The widespread idea during the nineteenth century that Indigenous peoples represented an earlier stage of sociocultural evolution provided the intellectual justification for Americans who coveted their land and demanded that they be forced to live on reservations or be killed if they resisted. In typical fashion, the editors of the Boston *Commercial Bulletin* regarded the triumph of "civilized" people over "savage" Indigenous peoples as historical "progress." In the selection printed here, they called for the acquisition and exploitation of the Indian lands in the vast western region of the United States. In the following years, the American government dispatched soldiers to round up the Indigenous peoples who roamed freely over their extensive hunting grounds and to force them onto small reservations where they could try to eke out an existence on marginal lands. Many Indigenous peoples reluctantly agreed to abandon their semi-nomadic lifestyle and to settle down as farmers on fixed reservations, whereas others decided to fight to protect their land and to preserve their culture that was under assault. But those who chose to resist were either captured or killed, and by 1890, only a few hundred thousand Indigenous peoples were left in the US.

The time has at length arrived when some decisive Indian policy must be inaugurated by the Federal Government, or the settlement and development of the great interior portion of our Continent must be indefinitely postponed. This is a question of the highest importance to all sections of the country, since all are directly interested in the opening up of new sources of wealth and commerce in that part of the national domain; and hence the government cannot too soon, or too earnestly, address itself to the work of solving it.

Civilized industry and enterprise, in their progress Westward, while seeking to open communications and fill up the gap between the great States of the

Atlantic and Pacific, have encountered a savage obstacle which disputes their passage. While the exigency was one of communication only, confined to a monthly, or semi-monthly, transportation of the mails, this obstacle could be endured, and passengers between California and the East were content to go by way of the Isthmus of Darien. But with the rapid growth of commerce, and the mineral development of the new territories lying upon both slopes of the Rocky Mountains, the extension of our railroad system into that great Western wilderness becomes a necessity. The work has well begun, and its early accomplishment promises the best results in increasing the area of freedom and civilization.

But just as we approach the confines of this mountain girt region, the untamed savage of the plains and prairies meets us and warns us off, claiming to be sole lord and monarch of all he surveys. He complains that the iron horse, driven by the pale face, intrudes upon his hunting grounds and frightens away his buffalo, and demands, as a condition of keeping the peace, and abstaining from the slaughter of defenseless immigrants and settlers, that further railroad building in the direction of his favorite haunts, upon the headwaters of the Missouri, Platte and Arkansas rivers, shall be abandoned.

Such was the modest demand made upon the Indian Commissioners, at their late council on the North Platte, by the Sioux, Cheyenne and Comanche Chiefs, to which Gen. Sherman replied with such firmness and severity. But the obstinate savages evidently have not yet yielded the point, and probably will not till dealt with in a different style from the mild diplomacy hitherto adopted. But the issue is plain: They must either be forcibly ejected from the path of progress, and made to live like civilized beings, by agricultural labor, upon fixed reservations, or they must be exterminated.

Source: *Boston Commercial Bulletin*, October 5, 1867, 8.

REVIEW QUESTIONS

Why did the editors argue that the time had come for the US government implement a decisive Indian policy?

How did the editors view the role of railroads in the development of the trans-Mississippi West?

How did the editors describe the conflict between the Indians and the pioneers moving westward?

Document 67

Jules Ferry, Colonialism and the Preservation of Capitalism, 1890

The acquisition to colonies in Indochina and Africa provoked a debate in France over the issue of empire. On one side, socialists and humanitarians argued that an imperial policy would mean enslavement rather than cultural improvement for the colonial people. These critics also charged that imperialism would benefit only a few businessmen and colonial administrators, while the great majority of French citizens would have to pay the cost of empire with the blood and money needed to maintain metropolitan control over distant territories. On the other side, bankers and manufacturers viewed colonial possessions not only as sources of raw material for French industry but also as markets for French capital and commodities. Narrowly preoccupied with their economic self-interest, business groups hoped that overseas colonies would provide immediate opportunities for profitable enterprise. But the most influential proponents of imperialism exhibited a broad concern for the long-range functioning of the entire French political economy. These system-conscious leaders, like Jules Ferry, advocated a program of overseas economic expansion to avoid the danger of radical social upheavals. After serving twice as the prime minister of France between 1880 and 1885, he asserted in a book published in 1890 that the preservation of capitalism depended on a policy of colonialism. Excerpts from his book follow.

Colonial policy is the child of industrialization. For wealthy nations where capital abounds and accumulates fast, where industry is continually expanding, and where even agriculture must be mechanized in order to survive, exports are essential for national prosperity. . . . Had it been possible to establish, among the leading industrial nations, some kind of rational division of labor, based on the natural resources and social aptitudes of the different producing countries, so that certain of them might engage in cotton and metallurgical manufacture, others in alcohol and sugar refining industries, and still others in woolen and silk production, Europe might not have had to seek markets for its products in lands beyond its borders. . . .

But today every nation wants to do its own spinning and weaving, forging and distilling. All of Europe refines sugar and tries to export it. With the arrival of the industrial giants, the United States and Germany, with a regenerated Italy, a Spain enriched by the investment of French capital, an enterprising Switzerland, and a growing Russia, the entire west has plunged down a slope from which there can be no return.

Beyond the Vosges and across the Atlantic, protectionism has increased the volume of manufactured goods, suppressed former outlets, and thrust the countries of Europe into a fierce competition for markets. To protect their home markets, nations have raised their tariff barriers. . . . The likely effect will be increased domestic competition and a general lowering of prices, profits, and wages.

The Protectionist system, unless accompanied by a serious colonial policy, is like a steam engine without a safety valve. An excess of capital invested in industry not only reduces profits on capital but also impedes the rise of wages. This is not an abstract law, but a phenomenon made of flesh and bones, driven by passions and willfulness. Social stability in this industrial age clearly depends on outlets for industrial goods. The economic crisis that has weighed so heavily on the workingmen of Europe since 1877, with its prolonged and frequent strikes, has simultaneously struck France, Germany, and England with a marked and persistent drop in exports. Europe is like a commercial firm whose business has been shrinking for a number of years. The European consumer-goods market is saturated; it is necessary to reach into other parts of the world for new consumers, or, at the dawn of the twentieth century, modern society will be bankrupt and will suffer destruction by some cataclysm whose consequences can scarcely be imagined. . . .

Colonial policy is an international manifestation of the eternal laws of competition. . . .

France is not weak. . . . Because it is strong, this great military state can support ten thousand men in Indochina. Because France is strong it must not abandon its role and rights as a great power. . . . A nation cannot be a great power by remaining bound to its own shores. . . .

Without compromising the security of the country, without sacrificing its past traditions and future aspirations, the Republicans have, in less than ten years, given France four kingdoms in Asia and Africa. . . . If the Republic had declared, like the doctrinaires of the Radical school, that the French nation ends at Marseilles, to whom would Tunisia, Indochina, Madagascar, and the Congo belong today?

Source: Jules Ferry, *Le Tonkin et la Mere-Patrie* (Paris: Victor-Harvard, 1890), 40–43 and 47–48. [Translated by Professor James R. Farr of Purdue University.]

REVIEW QUESTIONS

Why did Ferry believe that protectionism would be an inadequate policy?

Why did he think a colonial policy was necessary?

Why did he conclude that France must not abandon its status as a great power?

Document 68

Sergei Witte, A Memorandum on the Industrialization of Russia, 1899

When Sergei Witte became the Russian finance minister in 1892, he sponsored an ambitious program of industrialization. Witte hoped that an influx of foreign capital would enable Russia to catch up to the leading Western powers in economic growth and military strength within a decade. Under his direction, the Russian government gave private entrepreneurs huge subsidies and loans, big orders for goods, and large tax privileges. The government also erected high tariffs to protect Russian industries from foreign competition. In addition, the Russian government imposed heavy taxes on salt, alcohol, and sugar to obtain revenue needed to pay for large developmental projects, like the Trans-Siberian Railway, that would not yield immediate profits. Sometime early in 1899, Witte sent Tsar Nicholas II a secret memorandum on the subject of Russian industrialization. In his memorandum, excerpts printed here, Witte emphasized the need for protective tariffs and foreign capital to promote the industrial development and economic independence of Russia.

I was of course aware that there exist rather weighty objections to the protectionist system and to high tariffs, but I presumed that even the partisans of free trade must concede that it would be harmful in the extreme, from the perspective of the interests of the state, to abandon the protectionist system before those industries, for whose creation an entire generation has been paying the costs of a high tariff, were able to mature and consolidate themselves. . . .

The economic relations of Russia with Western Europe are completely similar to those of colonial lands to their metropolises. The latter view their colonies as a profitable market where they may freely sell the products of their labor and their industry, and from which they can extract with a strong hand the needed raw materials. This is how the states of Western Europe are building their economic might, and the conquest and defense of new colonies

222

are their principal instrument for this. Russia has been even up until now, to a certain extent, a hospitable colony for all the industrially developed states, generously supplying them with the cheap products of its land while paying dearly for their industrial products. But there is one core difference between the situation of Russia and that of colonies: Russia is a politically independent and strong power; it has the right and the ability not to want to be an eternal tributary of economically more developed states. . . . Russia itself seeks to be a metropolis—and on the soil of the people's labor, liberated from the confines of serfdom, our own national industry has begun to develop and promises to become a reliable counterweight to foreign industrial domination.

First of all, we should note that thanks to a consistent pursuit of the protectionist system in this country the fruits of our efforts have ripened. Manufacturing industries now number more than 30,000 factories and industrial plants annually produce goods valued at more than 2 billion rubles.

The influx of foreign capital, the Minister of Finance is deeply convinced, is the only means that we have to accelerate the development of our industry to the point where it is able to supply our country with an abundance of cheap products. . . .

The new sum of 100 million rubles which has flowed into our country this past year from abroad will lower by the laws of competition the rate of interest on all previous capital invested in industry, which totals billions of rubles. If the country pays out 10 million rubles in interest on that 100 million, it saves a much larger sum due to lower interest rates on the entire mass of capital at work in the economy. And such a massive cheapening of billions of rubles of national capital cannot but lead to a significant lowering of prices for all the products of our industry. We have cheap labor, huge natural resources, and only the high cost of capital prevents us from producing cheap goods. Let foreign capital help us . . . and we will be able to raise our industry to such a level that it will be able not only to provide cheap goods in abundance for domestic demand, but also provide goods for export. Even now we are approaching that goal, and the natural consequence of the changes we are undergoing will be that we will pay for the interest on the capital borrowed from Europe with the receipts from our exports to Asia. . . .

I have set out the major principles of the system of trade and industry pursued in Russia since the reign of Alexander III. Its point of departure was the protective tariff of 1891, lowered somewhat pursuant to trade agreements with France, Germany, Austria-Hungary and other countries. This system of tariffs had as its goal the creation in Russia of its own manufacturing, which would promote our economic, and consequently, our political independence and would allow us to establish more profitable international and domestic trade relations. . . .

If it would be particularly dangerous to rely on the competition of foreign products in the attempt to lower prices here, it would be possible to achieve this goal by allowing for the competition of foreign capital which, invested in Russia, could assist Russian productive forces, and thereby to stimulate our industrial development and to accelerate the process of accumulating our own capital.

Source: Vsepoddanneishii doklad ministra finansov S. Iu. Vitte Niklaiu II o neobkhodimosti ustanovit' i zatem neprelozhno priderzhivat'sia opredelennoi programmy torgovo-promyshlennoi politiki imperii. GA RF fond 601, opis' 1, delo 1026, listy 1–12. [This document from the Russian archives in Moscow has been translated for us by Professor Douglas R. Weiner of the University of Arizona.]

REVIEW QUESTIONS

How does Witte view the relationship between Russia and major industrial powers in Western Europe?

What is his attitude toward protective tariffs?

How does he view the role of foreign capital in Russia?

Document 69

John A. Hobson, The Economic Taproot of Imperialism, 1902

In 1902, shortly after the European powers had completed their colonization of Africa, John A. Hobson, a British economist, wrote a penetrating
critique of imperialism. He argued that imperialism was rooted in the unequal distribution of wealth in the advanced industrial countries. Influenced
by his views, European socialists argued that World War I, which began in
1914, was a rich man's war to and a poor man's fight to redraw the map of
the world. Hobson's analysis was recast in 1916 by Vladimir I. Lenin, the
Bolshevik leader in Russia, in his widely read book titled *Imperialism: The
Highest Stage of Capitalism*. Like Hobson, Eugene V. Debs, the president of
the Socialist Party of America, argued that if workers received higher wages
domestic consumption would match home production and there would be
no need to use military force to secure foreign outlets for surplus capital and
surplus commodities.

No mere array of facts and figures adduced to illustrate the economic nature
of the new Imperialism will suffice to dispel the popular delusion that the use
of national force to secure new markets by annexing fresh tracts of territory is
a sound and a necessary policy for an advanced industrial country like Great
Britain. . . .

It is open to Imperialists to argue thus: "We must have markets for our
growing manufactures, we must have new outlets for the investment of our
surplus capital and for the energies of the adventurous surplus of our population: such expansion is a necessity of life to a nation with our great and
growing powers of production. An ever larger share of our population is
devoted to the manufactures and commerce of towns, and is thus dependent
for life and work upon food and raw materials from foreign lands. During
the first three quarters of the nineteenth century we could do so without dif-

ficulty by a natural expansion of commerce with continental nations and our colonies, all of which were far behind us in the main arts of manufacture and the carrying trades. So long as England held a virtual monopoly of the world markets for certain important classes of manufactured goods, Imperialism was unnecessary. After 1870 this manufacturing and trading supremacy was greatly impaired: other nations, especially Germany, the United States, and Belgium, advanced with great rapidity, and while they have not crushed or even stayed the increase of our external trade, their competition made if more and more difficult to dispose of the full surplus of our manufactures at a profit. The encroachments made by these nations upon our old markets, even in our own possessions, made it most urgent that we should take energetic means to secure new markets. These new markets had to lie in hitherto undeveloped countries, chiefly in the tropics, where vast populations lived capable of growing economic needs which our manufacturers and merchants could supply. Our rivals were seizing and annexing territories for similar purposes, and when they had annexed them closed them to our trade. The diplomacy and arms of Great Britain had to be used in order to compel the owners of the new markets to deal with us: and experience showed that the safest means of securing and developing such markets is by establishing 'protectorates' or by annexation. . . .

Every improvement of the methods of production, every concentration of ownership and control, seems to accentuate the tendency. As one nation after another enters the machine economy and adopts advanced industrial methods, it becomes more difficult for its manufacturers, merchants, and financiers to dispose profitably of their economic resources, and they are tempted more and more to use their Governments in order to secure for their particular use some distant undeveloped country by annexation and protection.

The process, we may be told, is inevitable, and so it seems upon superficial inspection. Everywhere appear excessive powers of production, excessive capital in search of investment. It is admitted by all business men that the growth of the powers of production in their country exceeds the growth in consumption, that more goods can be produced than can be sold at a profit, and that more capital exists than can find remunerative investment.

It is this economic condition of affairs that forms the taproot of Imperialism. If the consuming public in this country raised its standard of consumption to keep pace with every rise of productive powers, there could be no excess of goods or capital clamorous to use Imperialism in order to find new markets. . . .

It is idle to attack Imperialism or Militarism as political expedients or policies unless the axe is laid at the economic root of the tree, and the classes for whose interest Imperialism works are shorn of the surplus revenues which seek this outlet.

Source: John A. Hobson, *Imperialism: A Study* (London: James Nesbit and Co., 1902). The excerpts are taken from chapter VI, The Economic Taproot of Imperialism, 76–99.

REVIEW QUESTIONS

Why does Hobson believe that Great Britain embarked on a colonial policy after 1870?

What does he identify as the taproot of imperialism?

Why does he think that advanced industrial countries can enjoy prosperity without dominating overseas territories?

Baron Yeiichi Shibusawa, The Rise of the Japanese Cotton Textile Industry, 1910

During the Meiji era (1868–1912), policy makers in Tokyo spearheaded a vigorous campaign to transform Japan into powerful and wealthy industrial country. Cotton manufacturing played an important role in the industrialization of Japan as it had previously done in Great Britain. Eager to promote the domestic production of yarn, the Japanese government purchased British textile machinery and constructed two small cotton mills with 2,000 spindles each to serve as models for the establishment of larger spinning factories. The government eventually sold these mills, and in 1883, private investors launched the Osaka Spinning Company with 10,500 spindles. The Osaka firm was quite profitable, and soon many other Japanese entrepreneurs established textile enterprises, which used ring spindles that were operated by women and children who worked long hours for low wages. Japanese investors also began establishing large integrated cotton factories that combined the two basic processes of spinning and weaving under one roof, and by 1914, Japan was exporting as much as 50 percent of its total output of cotton cloth. Baron Yeiichi Shibusawa played a leading part in the industrial development of Japan during the Meiji era. He served as president of the First National Bank, chairman of the Chamber of Commerce, and director of several of the largest business enterprises in Japan. In his discussion of Joint-Stock Enterprise in Japan printed here, Shibusawa notes that he was instrumental in starting the Osaka Spinning Company, the first large Japanese cotton factory.

In 1880–81 the Government, fully recognizing the necessity of encouraging this [cotton textile] industry, purchased machinery, and built and let model factories in the provinces of Mikawa, Owari, and Ise. The import of cotton yarn and cloth had been gradually increasing . . . so that the balance of foreign trade was lost, and it was thought very necessary to try to restore it. Cotton yarn and cloth, which form materials for daily use, represented a large portion of the country's imports, and it was deemed very important to establish manufactories of these articles in Japan.

In 1879 the writer was instrumental in starting the Osaka Spinning Company, but it was not until 1883 that its factories were completed and work begun. As this case is typical of others, it may be well to draw attention to the various causes that contributed to this long delay. The people had had no experience in establishing a large factory in this country, and on that account men had to be sent to England to investigate and study all the details of factory work. Again, surveys were made as to utilizing water power in Mikawa, Kii, and Yamashiro, but, the available water not being sufficient, it was decided to adopt steam power, and with a view to convenience in employing hands (male and female), and also to facilities of transport, the factory was ultimately established in Osaka. Yet again as regards material, cotton of home production was found by no means suitable or sufficient in quantity, and it became necessary to examine into the real condition of cotton in China, India, and some other Oriental countries, and to make arrangements for its import. At last it was settled to import cotton from America.

As the Osaka Spinning Company obtained good results and showed large profits, many enterprises in this line of industry have since been undertaken at Osaka and other places.

The Miye Spinning Company, the Settsu Spinning Company, the Hirano Spinning Company, the Kane-ga-Fuchi Spinning Company, and various other companies were started one after another, and enjoyed a full measure of prosperity. But as a consequence products increased so fast that supply often exceeded demand, and to avoid this evil, a market had to be found abroad. The best market was of course China, but that had been already monopolized by English and Indian yarns, therefore the spinners urged the necessity, if the competition was to be successful, of having cotton yarns free from export duty and raw cotton from import duty, and this the Government and the Diet recognized by abolishing the export duty on cotton yarn in 1894, and the import duty on raw cotton in 1896. . . .

The spinning industry has gradually progressed. Comparing its condition in 1895 with that in 1906, the number of factories increased from forty-seven to eighty-three; the industry, aggregate capital from 16,392,000 yen to 40,612,000 yen; the number of spindles in daily use from 518,736 to 1,425,406; and the quantity of cotton yarn from 18,437,011 kwamme (1 kwan = 8 lb.) to 46,187,845 kwamme. Besides this industry, silk and flax spinning enterprises have gradually progressed in recent years.

Owing to the development of the cotton industry, the condition of the import and export trade in this staple entirely changed. Between 1896 and 1906 the imports decreased from 11,372,000 yen to 4,656,000 yen, and the exports, on the contrary, increased from 4,029,000 yen to 35,303,000 yen. When we look back at a total export of 2364 yen in 1890, we may easily see what progress has been achieved. At the present time cotton yarns, together with habutae' (silk tissue), form the two chief staples of export next to raw silk.

It is natural that with the progress of spinning that of weaving also should have greatly developed, as these two industries are very closely connected. Statistics show that in 1895 the cotton piece-goods produced were 63,420,000 pieces (valued at 35,650,469 yen) . . . and in 1905 the cotton piece-goods increased to 90,663,000 pieces (value 65,888,510 yen). . . .

Source: Count Shigenobu Okuma, *Fifty Years of New Japan*, 2nd ed., ed. Marcus B. Huish (London: Smith, Elder & Co., 1910), 1:479–82.

REVIEW QUESTIONS

What part did the Japanese government play in establishing a domestic cotton textile industry?

Where did the Osaka Spinning Company obtain its supply of raw cotton?

How did the Japanese government facilitate the export of cotton yarn to China?

Document 71

Emiliano Zapata, The Plan of Ayala, 1911

The Mexican Revolution began in November 1910 when Francisco I. Madero, a wealthy landowner who represented provincial elite families in northeastern Mexico, decided to overthrow Porfirio Díaz who had seized power in 1876 and opened the country to foreign investment, especially from the US. As American capital poured into Mexico, peasants were expelled from their farms, and as the paso declined in value relative to the dollar, provincial elites found it increasingly difficult to purchase land. Madero sought to build a wide base of support by making vague proposals, contained in his Plan of San Luis Potosí, for land reform. Prospects for land redistribution prompted Emiliano Zapata and Francisco "Pancho" Villa to join the rebellion, and their peasant followers soon started attacking and occupying large agricultural estates. But after Madero was elected president, he refused to satisfy peasant demands for land. As a result, Madero lost the support of Zapata and his peasant followers in central Mexico, and in November 1911, Zapata and his colleagues issued The Plan of Ayala as their revolutionary manifesto against Madero. The unequal distribution of land remained a central issue throughout the Mexican Revolution. Excerpts from the plan appear here.

The undersigned, constituted into a Revolutionary Junta to sustain and carry out the promises to the country by the Revolution of 20 November 1910, solemnly declare before the civilized world which sits in judgment on us, and before the Nation to which we belong and which we love, the propositions we have formulated to do away with the tyranny that oppresses us and to redeem the Fatherland from the dictatorships that are imposed upon us, which are outlined in the following plan:

Taking into consideration that the Mexican people, led by don Francisco I. Madero, went out to shed their blood to reconquer liberties and vindicate their rights which had been trampled upon, not so that one man could seize power, violating the sacred principles that he swore to defend with the slogan "Effective Suffrage and No Reelection," thereby insulting the faith, cause and liberties of the people. . . . Taking into account that the so-called chief of the Liberating Revolution of Mexico, don Francisco I. Madero, due to his great weakness and lack of integrity, did not bring to a happy conclusion the Revolution that he began with the help of God and of the people, since he left intact the majority of the governing powers and corrupt elements of oppression from the dictatorial Government of Porfirio Diaz, which are not and can never in any way be the representation of the National sovereignty, and that, being terrible enemies of ourselves and of the principles that we defend, are causing the ills of the country and opening new demands in the breast of the Fatherland, making it drink its own blood; taking also into account the aforementioned don Francisco I. Madero, current president of the Republic, tried to avoid fulfilling the promises he made to the nation in the Plan of San Luis Potosi, . . . nullifying, persecuting, imprisoning, or killing the revolutionary elements who helped him occupy the high post of president of the Republic. . . .

Francisco I. Madero is disavowed as Chief of the Revolution and as President of the Republic for the reasons expressed above. We shall bring about the overthrow of this functionary.

. . . .

The Revolutionary Junta of the State of Morelos manifests to the Nation, under formal protest, that it adopts the Plan of San Luis Potosi as its own, with the additions that shall be expressed below, for the benefit of the oppressed peoples, and will make itself the defender of the principles that they defend until victory or death. . . .

The Revolutionary Junta of the State of Morelos will not admit transactions or agreements until it has brought about the defeat of the dictatorial elements of Porfirio Diaz and of Francisco I. Madero, for the Nation is tired of false men and traitors who make promises like liberators, and upon attaining power forget those promises and become tyrants.

As an additional part of our plan, we make it known: that the lands, forests and waters that have been usurped by the hacendados [large landowners], cientificos [government functionaries] or caciques [local officials] in the shadow of venal justice, will henceforth enter into the possession of the villages or of citizens who have titles corresponding to those properties, and who have been despoiled through the bad faith of our oppressors, and they shall maintain that possession with weapon in hand, and the usurpers who believe they have rights to those lands will be heard by the special tribunals that will be established upon the triumph of the Revolution.

In view of the fact that the immense majority of Mexican villages and citizens own no more land than that which they tread upon, and are unable in any way to better their social condition or dedicate themselves to industry or agriculture, because the lands, forests, and waters are monopolized in only a few hands; for this reason, we expropriate without previous indemnization one third of those monopolies from the powerful proprietors, to the end that the villages and citizens of Mexico should obtain ejidos [communal farm lands], colonias [urban neighborhoods], and fundos legales [endowments of land] for the villages, or fields for sowing or laboring, and this shall correct the lack of prosperity and increase the well-being of the Mexicans.

The hacendados, cientificos or caciques who directly or indirectly oppose the present Plan, shall have their properties nationalized and two thirds of those properties shall be given as indemnizations of war, pensions to widows and orphans of the victims who are killed in the struggles surrounding the present Plan.

. . . .

Once the Revolution that we are making has triumphed, a junta of the principal revolutionary chiefs of the different States will name or designate an interim President of the Republic, who will convoke the elections for the organization of federal powers.

. . . .

Mexicans: consider the deviousness and bad faith of a man who is shedding blood in a scandalous manner, because he is incapable of governing; consider that his system of Government is tying up the fatherland and trampling upon our institutions with the brute force of bayonets; so that the very weapons we took to bring him to Power, we now turn against him for failing to keep his promises to the Mexican people and for having betrayed the Revolution he began; we are not personalists, we are partisans of principles and not of men!

Mexican people, support this Plan with weapons in your hands, and bring prosperity and welfare to the Fatherland.

Source: Gilbert M. Joseph and Timothy J. Henderson, *The Mexican Reader: History, Culture, and Politics* (Durham, NC: Duke University Press, 2002), 339–43. [The Plan of Ayala was translated by Timothy J. Henderson.]

REVIEW QUESTIONS

How did Zapata and his followers view Madero?

How did they plan to create a more equitable distribution of land?

How did they intend to treat landowners who opposed their plan?

Rosa Luxemburg, Women's Suffrage and the Class Struggle, 1912

Born in Poland in 1871 when it was part of the Russian Empire, Rosa Luxemburg was a brilliant student who studied law and political economy at the University of Zurich where in 1898 she received a PhD. Luxemburg moved to Berlin and promptly joined the Social Democratic Party of Germany, and inspired by the Russian Revolution in 1905, she began advocating a general strike to mobilize industrial workers and to spread socialism throughout Europe. When the Social Democratic Party backed the German government at the outbreak of World War I in 1914, she helped found the Spartacus League that sought to end the war by overthrowing the capitalist regimes in the belligerent countries and establish governments that represented the working class. Luxemburg became a sophisticated Marxist theoretician who stressed democratic principles, and in 1918 she criticized Vladimir Lenin for his dictatorial rule in Russia. As revealed in her speech excerpted here, Luxemburg was a fierce champion of women's rights not only to achieve gender equality but also to liberate both the male and female members of the working class.

More than a hundred fifty thousand women are organized in unions and are among the most active troops in the economic struggle of the proletariat. Many thousands of politically organized women have rallied to the banner of Social Democracy. . . . Women's suffrage is one of the vital issues on the platform of Social Democracy. . . .

In truth, our state is interested in keeping the vote from working women and from them alone. It rightly fears they will threaten the traditional institutions of class rule, for instance militarism (of which no thinking proletarian woman can help being a deadly enemy), monarchy, the systematic robbery of duties and taxes on groceries, etc. Women's suffrage is a horror and abomination for the present capitalist state because behind it stand millions of women who would strengthen the enemy within, i.e., revolutionary Social Democracy. If it were a matter of bourgeois ladies voting, the capitalist state could expect nothing but effective support for the reaction. Most of those bourgeois women who act like lionesses in the struggle against "male prerogatives" would trot like docile lambs in the camp of conservative and clerical reaction if they had suffrage. Indeed, they would certainly be a good deal more reactionary than the male part of their class. Aside from the few who have jobs or professions, the women of the bourgeoisie do not take part in social production. They are nothing but co-consumers of the surplus value their men extort from the proletariat. They are parasites of the parasites of the social body. And consumers are usually even more rabid and cruel in defending their "right" to a parasite's life than the direct agents of class rule and exploitation. . . . The women of the property-owning classes will always fanatically defend the exploitation and enslavement of the working people by which they indirectly receive the means for their socially useless existence.

Economically and socially, the women of the exploiting classes are not an independent segment of the population. Their only social function is to be tools of the natural propagation of the ruling classes. By contrast, the women of the proletariat are economically independent. They are productive for society like the men. By this I do not mean their bringing up children or their housework which helps men support their families on scanty wages. This kind of work is not productive in the sense of the present capitalist economy no matter how enormous an achievement the sacrifices and energy spent. . . . As long as capitalism and the wage system rule, only that kind of work is considered productive which produces surplus value, which creates capitalist profit. . . .

For, exactly from this point of view, the proletarian women's claim to equal political rights is anchored in firm economic ground. Today, millions of proletarian women create capitalist profit like men-in factories, workshops, on farms, in home industry, offices, stores. They are therefore productive in the strictest scientific sense of our present society. Every day enlarges the hosts of women exploited by capitalism. Every new progress in industry or technology creates new places for women in the machinery of capitalist profiteering. And thus, every day and every step of industrial progress adds a new stone to the firm foundation of women's equal political rights. . . .

Considering all this, the proletarian woman's lack of political rights is a vile injustice. . . . However, Social Democracy does not use the argument of "injustice." . . . We do not depend on the justice of the ruling classes, but solely on the revolutionary power of the working masses and on the course of social development which prepares the ground for this power. . . .

Because of the female proletariat, general, equal, direct suffrage for women would immensely advance and intensify the proletarian class struggle. This is why bourgeois society abhors and fears women's suffrage. And this is why we want and will achieve it. Fighting for women's suffrage, we will also hasten the coming of the hour when the present society falls in ruins under the hammer strokes of the revolutionary proletariat.

Source: Dick Howard, ed. *Selected Political Writings, Rosa Luxemburg*, Monthly Review Press, 1971. Speech: May 12, 1912 (at the Second Social Democratic Women's Rally, Stuttgart, Germany).

Source: Selected Political Writings, Rosa Luxemburg. Edited and introduced by Dick Howard. Monthly Review Press © 1971.

Translated: Rosmarie Waldrop (from the German Ausgewählte Reden und Schriften, 2 (Berlin: Dietz Verlag, 1951, 433–41). Transcription/Markup: Brian Baggins.

Monthly Review Press © 1971. Published here by the Marxists Internet Archive (marxists.org, 2003) with permission from Monthly Review Press.

REVIEW QUESTIONS

Why did Luxemburg believe that capitalists did not fear if upper-class women obtained the right to vote?

Why did she believe that capitalists feared that working-class women would win the right to vote?

How did she distinguish the function in capitalist societies of working within and outside household?

Document 73

William G. McAdoo and Robert Lansing, The American Decision to Make Loans to the Allied Powers, 1915

When World War I began in August 1914, President Woodrow Wilson declared that the US would remain neutral, and Secretary of State William Jennings Bryan issued a statement that prohibited American loans to belligerent countries. The British and French paid for essential American supplies by selling whatever they could: first goods, then gold, and finally their investments in the US. As their gold supplies and foreign assets dwindled, the British and French hoped to buy goods on credit from the US. Both Secretary of the Treasury William G. McAdoo and newly appointed Secretary of State Robert Lansing urged President Wilson to remove the ban on American loans to belligerent nations. In October 1915, Wilson decided to authorize American bankers to make loans to the Allies after he received the following letters, excerpted here, from these top officials. Wilson eventually decided that he would not be able to exercise a decisive influence at the peace table unless the US entered the war and helped turn the tide of battle in favor of the Allies. After the US declared war in April 1917, the American government began providing Britain and France loans that ultimately totaled nearly $10 billion. In July 1917, Wilson told Colonel Edward M. House, his top foreign policy adviser, that the Allies would become so indebted to the US that he would be able to dominate the peace settlement.

Secretary of the Treasury McAdoo to President Wilson, 21 August 1915:
You know how loath I am always to burden you with Treasury affairs, but matters of such great importance have arisen in connection with the financing of our export trade that you ought to know the facts.

Great Britain is, and always has been, our best customer. Since the war began, her purchases and those of her Allies (France, Russia, and Italy) have enormously increased. Food products constitute the greater part of these purchases, but war munitions, which as you know embrace not only arms and ammunition, but saddles, horses, and mules and a variety of other things, are a big item. The high prices for food products have brought great prosperity to our farmers, while the purchases of war munitions have stimulated industry and have set factories going to full capacity throughout the great manufacturing districts, while the reduction of imports and their actual cessation in some cases, have caused new industries to spring up and others to be enlarged. Great Prosperity is coming. It is in large measure here already. It will be tremendously increased if we can extend reasonable credits to our customers. The balance of trade is so largely in our favor and will grow even larger if trade continues, that we cannot demand payments in gold alone, without eventually exhausting the gold reserves of our best customers, which would ruin their credit and stop their trade with us. They must begin to cut their purchases from us to the lowest limit, unless we extend to them reasonable credit. Our prosperity is dependent on our continued and enlarged foreign trade. To preserve that we must do everything we can to assist our customers to buy.

We have repeatedly declared that it is lawful for our citizens to manufacture and sell to belligerents munitions of war. It is lawful commerce and being lawful is entitled to the same treatment at the hands of our bankers, in financing it, as our other part of lawful commerce. . . .

It is imperative for England to establish a large credit in this country. She will need at least $500,000,000. She can't get this in any way, at the moment, that seems feasible, except by the sale of short-time Government notes. Here she encounters the obstacle presented by Mr. [former Secretary of State] Bryan's letter of June 20, 1915 to Senator Stone in which it is stated that "war loans in this country were disapproved because inconsistent with the spirit of neutrality" etc., and "this Government has not been advised that general loans have been made by foreign governments in this country since *the President expressed his wish that loans of this character should not be made.*" The underscored part is the hardest hurdle of this entire letter. Large banking houses here, which have the ability to finance a large loan, will not do so or even attempt to do so, in the face of this declaration. We have tied our hands so that we cannot help ourselves or help our best customers. France and Russia are in the same boat. Each, especially France, needs a large credit here.

The declaration seems to me most illogical and inconsistent. We approve and encourage sales of supplies to England and others but we disapprove the creation by them of credit balances here to finance their lawful and welcome purchases. We must find some way to give them needed credits but there is no way, I fear, unless this declaration can be modified. . . .

I wish you would think about this so we may discuss it when I see you. To maintain our prosperity, we must finance it. Otherwise it may stop and that would be disastrous. . . .

Secretary of State Lansing to President Wilson, 6 September 1915:

My Dear Mr. President: Doubtless Secretary McAdoo has discussed with you the necessity of floating government loans for the belligerent nations, which are purchasing such great quantities of *goods in this country, in order to avoid a serious financial situation which will not only affect them but* this country as well. . . .

If the European countries cannot find means to pay for the excess of goods sold to them over those purchased from them, they will have to stop buying and our present export trade will shrink proportionately. The result will be restriction of outputs, industrial depression, idle capital and idle labor, numerous failures, financial demoralization, and general unrest and suffering among the laboring classes. . . .

I believe that Secretary McAdoo is convinced and I agree with him that there is only one means of avoiding this situation which would so seriously affect economic conditions in this country, and that is the flotation of large bond issues by the belligerent governments. Our financial institutions have the money to loan and wish to do so. On account of the great balance of trade in our favor the proceeds of these loans would be expended here. The result would be maintenance of the credit of the borrowing nations based on their gold reserve, a continuance of our commerce at its present volume and industrial activity with the consequent employment of capital and labor and national prosperity.

The difficulty is—and this is what Secretary McAdoo came to see me about—that the Government early in the war announced that it considered "war loans" to be contrary to "the true spirit of neutrality." A declaration to this effect was given to the press about August 15, 1914, by Secretary Bryan. . . . Can we afford to let a declaration as to our conception of "the true spirit of neutrality" made in the first days of the war stand in the way of our national interests which seem to be seriously threatened?

Source: *Hearings Before the Special Committee Investigating the Munitions Industry*, 74th Cong., 2d. Sess., pt. 26 (Washington, DC: Government Printing Office, 1937), 8123–25; and *Foreign Relations of the United States: The Lansing Papers* (Washington, DC: Government Printing Office, 1939), 1:144–47.

REVIEW QUESTIONS

Why did Bryan oppose American loans to belligerent countries?

How did World War I affect the balance of payments between the US and the European nations?

How did McAdoo and Lansing view the relationship between American exports and the economy of the US?

Document 74

Mohandas K. Gandhi, A Condemnation of British Imperialism in India, 1922

Mohandas K. Gandhi was born in western India in 1869 and raised by Hindu parents. In the aftermath of World War I, he launched a nonviolent campaign that advocated passive resistance to British rule in India. In 1922, British officials arrested Gandhi and accused him of having written seditious newspaper articles. Gandhi made a sweeping condemnation of British rule in India in the statement, excerpted here, that he gave at his trial. Though he was found guilty and sentenced to six years in prison, Gandhi had established himself as the moral leader of the nationalist movement in India. In 1930, after embracing the goal of complete Indian independence from the British Empire, Gandhi decided to produce salt in violation of British law with the aim of winning a large following among Hindus and Muslims alike. His arrest provoked strikes throughout India, and soon Indian prisons were packed with tens of thousands of protesters. In 1942, in the midst of World War II, Gandhi launched his last great passive resistance campaign, which led to the arrest of some sixty thousand Indian demonstrators. The British decided when the war ended three years later that the burdens of empire were beginning to outweigh the benefits and that they could no longer afford to retain possession of India. Gandhi fervently hoped that an independent India would be a united country with a mixed population of Muslims and Hindus. When the British departed in 1947, however, India and Pakistan became two separate nations as desired by the Muslim League.

I owe it perhaps to the Indian public and to the public in England, to placate which this prosecution is mainly taken up that I should explain why from a staunch loyalist and co-operator, I have become an uncompromising disaffectionist and Non-Co-operator. To the Court too I should say why I plead guilty to the charge of promoting disaffection towards the Government established by law in India. . . .

I came reluctantly to the conclusion that the British connection had made India more helpless than she ever was before, politically and economically. A disarmed India has no power of resistance against any aggressor if she wanted to engage in an armed conflict with him. So much is this the case that some of our best men consider that India must take generations before she can achieve the Dominion status. She has become so poor that she has little power of resisting famines. Before the British advent, India spun and wove in her millions of cottages just the supplement she needed for adding to her meager agricultural resources. This cottage industry, so vital for India's existence, has been ruined by incredibly heartless and inhuman processes as described by English witnesses. Little do town-dwellers know how the semi-starved masses of India are slowly sinking to lifelessness. Little do they know that their miserable comfort represents the brokerage they get for the work they do for the foreign exploiter, that the profits and the brokerage are sucked from the masses. Little do they realize that the Government established by law in British India is carried on for this exploitation of the masses. No sophistry, no jugglery in figures can explain away the evidence the skeletons in many villages present to the naked eye. I have no doubt whatsoever that both England and the town-dwellers of India will have to answer, if there is a God above, for this crime against humanity which is perhaps unequalled in history. The law itself in this country has been used to serve the foreign exploiter. My unbiased examination of the Punjab Martial Law cases has led me to believe that at least ninety-five per cent of convictions were wholly bad. My experience of political cases in India leads me to the conclusion that in nine out of every ten the condemned men were totally innocent. Their crime consisted in love of their country. In ninety-nine cases out of a hundred, justice has been denied to Indians as against Europeans in the Courts of India. This is not an exaggerated picture. It is the experience of almost every Indian who has anything to do with such cases. In my opinion, the administration of the law is thus prostituted consciously or unconsciously for the benefit of the exploiter. . . .

In fact, I believe that I have rendered a service to India and to England by showing in [non-co-]operation the way out of the unnatural state in which both are living. In my humble opinion, non-co-operation with evil is as much a duty as is co-operation with good. But in the past, non-co-operation has been deliberately expressed in violence to the evil-doer. I am endeavoring to show to my countrymen that violent non-co-operation only multiplies evil and that as evil can only be sustained by violence, withdrawal of support of evil requires complete abstention from violence. Non-violence implies voluntary submission to the penalty for non-co-operation with evil. I am here, therefore, to invite and submit cheerfully to the highest penalty that can be inflicted upon me for what in law is deliberate crime and what appears to me to be the highest duty of a citizen. The only course open to you, the Judge and the Assessors, is either to resign your posts and thus dissociate yourselves from evil if you feel that the law you are called upon to administer is an evil and that in reality I am innocent, or to inflict on me the severest penalty if you believe that the system and the law you are assisting to administer are good for the people of this country and that my activity is therefore injurious to the public weal.

Source: *Speeches and Writings of M.K. Gandhi*, 3rd ed. (Madras: G. A. Nate-
    san & Co., 1922), 751–57.

REVIEW QUESTIONS

According to Gandhi, why did India become impoverished?

How does he say that Indians were treated in British courts?

Why did he willingly submit to the penalty for his refusal to cooperate with
    British laws?

Document 75

Adolf Hitler, German War Aims Regarding Poland and Russia, 1939

At a conference with his leading generals on August 22, 1939, Adolf Hitler explained his plans to depopulate Poland and Russia to make room for German settlers in conquered eastern territories. On the next day, Nazi Germany signed a nonaggression pact with the Soviet Union. Hitler regarded his deal with Stalin as a temporary arrangement that would dissuade Britain and France from coming to the aid of Poland. When German forces invaded Poland on September 1, 1939, the British and French declared war on Germany, but they declined to dispatch troops to defend Poland. Germany launched a massive assault on the western front in spring 1940, and after fighting for six weeks, France sued for peace. Hoping to avoid a two-front war, Hitler attempted to conclude a peace settlement with England, but the British rejected his peace overtures. And in June 1941, Hitler order his troops to invade the Soviet Union. An American journalist obtained a report, probably from a disgruntled German official, on the speech that Hitler had made to his generals prior to the German invasion of Poland. The journalist gave a copy of the report, excerpted here, to a British diplomat.

Decision to attack Poland was arrived at in spring. Originally there was fear that because of the political constellation we would have to strike at the same time against England, France, Russia and Poland. This risk too we should have had to take. [Field Marshall] Göring had demonstrated to us that his Four-Year Plan [to reduce German dependence on overseas resources] is a failure and that we are at the end of our strength, if we do not achieve victory in a coming war.

Since the autumn of 1938 and since I have realised that Japan will not go with us unconditionally and that Mussolini is endangered by that nitwit of a King and the treacherous scoundrel of a Crown Prince, I decided to go with

Stalin. After all there are only three great statesmen in the world, Stalin, I and Mussolini. Mussolini is the weakest, for he has been able to break the power neither of the crown nor of the Church. Stalin and I are the only ones who visualise the future. So in a few weeks hence, I shall stretch out my hand to Stalin at the common German-Russian frontier and with him undertake to re-distribute the world.

Our strength lies in our quickness and in our brutality; Genghis Khan has sent millions of women and children into death knowingly and with a light heart. History sees in him only the great founder of States. As to what the weak Western European civilisation asserts about me, that is of no account. I have given the command and I shall shoot everyone who utters one word of criticism, for the goal to be obtained in the war is not that of reaching certain lines but of physically demolishing the opponent. And so for the present only in the East I have put my death-head formations [SS combat units] in place with the command relentlessly and without compassion to send into death many women and children of Polish origin and language. Only thus can we gain the living space that we need. Who after all is today speaking about the destruction of the Armenians?

Colonel-General von Brauchitsch has promised me to bring the war against Poland to a close within a few weeks. Had he reported to me that he needs two years or even only one year, I should not have given the command to march and should have allied myself temporarily with England instead of Russia for we cannot conduct a long war. To be sure a new situation has arisen. I experienced those poor worms [French Premier] Daladier and [British Prime Minister] Chamberlain in Munich. They will be too cowardly to attack. They won't go beyond a blockade. Against that we have our autarchy and the Russian raw materials.

Poland will be depopulated and settled with Germans. My pact with the Poles was merely conceived of as a gaining of time. As for the rest, gentlemen, the fate of Russia will be exactly the same as I am now going through with in the case of Poland. After Stalin's death—he is a very sick man—we will break the Soviet Union.

The opportunity is as favorable as never before. . . .

For you, gentlemen, fame and honour are beginning as they have not since centuries. Be hard, be without mercy, act more quickly and brutally than the others. The citizens of Western Europe must tremble with horror. That is the most human way of conducting a war. For it scares the others off. . . .

The speech was received with enthusiasm. Goring jumped on a table, thanked bloodthirstily and made bloodthirsty promises. He danced like a wild man. The few that had misgivings remained quiet. . . .

During the meal which followed Hitler said he must act this year as he was not likely to live very long. His successor however would no longer be able to carry this out. Besides, the situation would be a hopeless one in two years at the most.

Source: *British Foreign Policy, 1919–1939*, 2nd Series, 1939, VII:258–60.

REVIEW QUESTIONS

How did Hitler explain his decision to make a deal with Stalin?

How long did he predict that it would take for German troops to subdue Poland?

Why did he argue that German troops should act with great brutality?

Document 76

Dean G. Acheson, The American Need for Overseas Markets, 1944

Following the stock market crash on wall Street in 1929, the US plunged into the decade-long Great Depression. Business executives shut down factories and laid off workers as demand for consumer goods dried up. Economic recovery did not come until after the onset of World War II in 1939 when American factories began receiving orders for a vast array of weapons and munitions from the US government and the Allied nations. The military spending sparked a revival of industrial production and created jobs for millions of those without work. But policy makers in Washington feared that when American factories converted to producing civilian goods after the war the US would suffer from the twin problems of overproduction and unemployment. During hearings conducted by the Special Committee on Post-War Economic Policy and Planning in the US House of Representatives, Assistant Secretary of State Dean G. Acheson presented his views on the need to expand American foreign trade. Acheson stressed his belief, during his testimony excerpted here, that overseas markets would be necessary to assure the successful functioning of capitalism in the US. While serving as undersecretary of state between 1945 and 1947, Acheson promoted the Marshall Plan, which provided European countries with grants needed to purchase American goods.

Testimony of Dean G. Acheson on 30 November 1944

MR. WORLEY. . . .
Would you give us briefly the reasons why you believe we should develop our foreign trade?

MR. ACHESON. Yes; I shall be glade to, Mr. Chairman.

I think the way to approach the development of our foreign trade is to start by looking at our own situation. . . .

In the first place, our own interest is to maintain the full employment which we have at the present time and expand it sufficiently to absorb the twelve million or more men and women who will come back from the services.

If we do not do that, it seems clear that we are in for a very bad time, so far as the economic and social position of this country is concerned.

We cannot go through another 10 years like the 10 years at the end of the twenties and the beginning of the thirties, without having the most far-reaching consequences upon our economic and social system.

MR. WALTER. When you speak of expanding employment have you in mind the many people who are temporarily employed and would not be employed were it not for the fact that we are at war?

MR. ACHESON. Yes; I have that in mind, Mr. Congressman, but when you take out the number temporarily employed and consider the ones who are coming back from the armed services, you will find we have a net addition to take care of.

Many of the people now employed are employed on a part-time basis, many women are working on a part-time basis, but you will find, I believe, that when everybody who does not have to work and is working for patriotic reasons goes back to his other activities, you will still have people to employ.

When we look at the problem, we may say it is a problem of markets. You don't have a problem of production. The United States has unlimited creative energy. The important thing is markets.

We have got to see that what the country produces is used and sold under financial arrangements which make its production possible.

So far as I know, no group which has studied this problem, and there have been many, as you know, has ever believed that our domestic markets could absorb our entire production under our present system.

You must look to foreign markets.

Some estimates go as high a $10,000,000 of exports a year.

We could argue for quite a while that under a different system in this country you could use the entire production of the country in the United States.

MR. WORLEY. What do you mean by that?

MR. ACHESON. I take it the Soviet Union could use its entire production internally.

If you wish to control the entire trade and income of the United States, which means the life of the people, you could probably fix it so that everything produced here would be consumed here, but that would completely change our Constitution, our relations to property, human liberty, our very conception of law.

And nobody contemplates that. Therefore, you find you must look to other markets and those markets are abroad.

It happens that these other markets are quite as anxious for our goods as we are to sell them. They always have been to some extent, but now that is true as never before.

This war has created a colossal demand such as has never existed before. But it is only a wish and not an economic demand unless there is purchasing power put behind it.

MR. WORLEY. Isn't there very little purchasing power behind these demands?

MR. ACHESEON. There could be very considerable purchasing power behind the demand. . . .

MR. WALTER. But in the period during which they are rebuilding they are, of course, going to manufacture and produce. Then, of course, comes the problem of accepting those goods in competition with our own manufactures.

MR. ACHESON. I understand that problem and what I am trying to do is to bring that out in answer to the chairman's question. But the first thing that I want to bring out is that we need these markets for the output of the United States.

If I am wrong about that, then all the argument falls by the wayside, but my contention is that we cannot have full employment and prosperity in the United States without the foreign markets. That is point one, and if anyone wants to challenge me on that we will go over it again.

MR. WORLEY. I think we are agreed on that.

MR. ACHESON. How do we go about getting it? What you have to do at the outset is to make credit available. . . .

Take the Greeks, the Poles, or the British. At the end of this war there will be a period of 3 or 4 years when what they have to export will not equal what they have to import immediately to eat and live. That is the field of short-term credits.

You have to find some way to get over that, and that is important for our business, also, because we will be selling much of that material.

MR. WORLEY. In that connection, Mr. Acheson, short-term credit by private capital or government?

MR. ACHESON. I don't believe private capital can possibly do it.

MR. WORLEY. Why not?

MR. ACHESON. I don't think there is enough private capital willing to engage in that activity, which is quite risky. There will be a lot of losses. The interest rates which private lenders will require in these circumstances will be too high. . . .

Source: US House of Representatives, Hearings before the Subcommittee on Foreign Trade and Shipping, Special Committee on Post-War Economic

Policy and Planning, 79th Congress 1st Session (Washington, DC: Government Printing Office, 1945), 1972–98.

REVIEW QUESTIONS

Why did Acheson believe that American prosperity depended on foreign trade?

What did he think would happen if the US adopted a policy of economic isolation?

Why did he argue that the American government would have to offer credit to foreign nations?

Document 77

Ho Chi Minh, Declaration of Vietnamese Independence, 1945

After struggling for years against the French and then the Japanese, Ho Chi Minh and his Vietminh colleagues quickly grasped the opportunity to attain independence for Vietnam when World War II ended. On August 16, 1945, two days after Japan surrendered to the US, Ho issued a call for a general uprising, and within a week the, Vietminh had gained control of the entire country. Then the Vietminh, after pressuring the French puppet Emperor Bao Dai to abdicate his throne, decided to establish the Democratic Republic of Vietnam (DRV). On September 2, 1945, speaking before a crowd of 500,000 people assembled in Hanoi, Ho proclaimed Vietnamese independence. Excerpts from his Declaration of Independence are printed here. Ho was hopeful that American leaders would abide by their promise, enunciated four years previously in the Atlantic Charter, to support the democratic principle of national self-determination. But President Truman and his State Department advisers refused to recognize the DRV, and they decided to support the French military effort, which began in earnest in December 1946, to reconquer Vietnam. By the time President Eisenhower was in the White House in January 1953, the US was supplying about 80 percent of the French military budget in Vietnam.

All men are created equal. They are endowed by their Creator with certain inalienable rights, among them are Life, Liberty, and the pursuit of Happiness.

This immortal statement was made in the Declaration of Independence of the United States of America in 1776. In a broader sense, this means: All the peoples on the earth are equal from birth, all the peoples have a right to live, to be happy and free.

The Declaration of the French Revolution made in 1791 on the Rights of Man and the Citizen also states: "All men are born free and with equal rights, and must always remain free and have equal rights."

Those are undeniable truths.

Nevertheless, for more than eighty years, the French imperialists, abusing the standard of Liberty, Equality, and Fraternity, have violated our Fatherland and oppressed our fellow-citizens. They have acted contrary to the ideals of humanity and justice.

In the field of politics, they have deprived our people of every democratic liberty.

They have enforced inhuman laws; they have set up three distinct political regimes in the North, the Center and the South of Vietnam in order to wreck our national unity and prevent our people from being united.

They have built more prisons than schools. They have mercilessly slain our patriots; they have drowned our uprisings in rivers of blood.

They have fettered public opinion; they have practiced obscurantism against our people.

To weaken our race they have forced us to use opium and alcohol.

In the field of economics, they have fleeced us to the backbone, impoverished our people, and devastated our land.

They have robbed us of our rice fields, our mines, our forests, and our raw materials. They have monopolized the issuing of bank-notes and the export trade.

They have invented numerous unjustifiable taxes and reduced our people, especially our peasantry, to a state of extreme poverty.

They have hampered the prospering of our national bourgeoisie; they have mercilessly exploited our workers.

In the autumn of 1940, when the Japanese Fascists violated Indochina's territory to establish new bases in their fight against the Allies, the French imperialists went down on their bended knees and handed over our country to them.

Thus, from that date, our people were subjected to the double yoke of the French and the Japanese. Their sufferings and miseries increased. The result was that from the end of last year to the beginning of this year, from Quang Tri province to the North of Vietnam, more than two million of our fellow-citizens died from starvation. On March 9, the French troops were disarmed by the Japanese. The French colonialists either fled or surrendered showing that not only were they incapable of "protecting" us, but that, in the span of five years, they had twice sold our country to the Japanese. . . .

After the Japanese had surrendered to the Allies, our whole people rose to regain our national sovereignty and to found the Democratic Republic of Vietnam.

The truth is that we have wrested our independence from the Japanese and not from the French.

The French have fled, the Japanese have capitulated, Emperor Bao Dai has abdicated. Our people have broken the chains which for nearly a century have fettered them and have won independence for the Fatherland. Our people at the same time have overthrown the monarchic regime that has reigned supreme for dozens of centuries. In its place has been established the present Democratic Republic.

For these reasons, we, members of the Provisional Government, representing the whole Vietnamese people, declare that from now on we break off all relations of a colonial character with France; we repeal all the international obligation that France has so far subscribed to on behalf of Vietnam and we abolish all the special rights the French have unlawfully acquired in our Fatherland.

The whole Vietnamese people, animated by a common purpose, are determined to fight to the bitter end against any attempt by the French colonialists to reconquer their country.

We are convinced that the Allied nations which at Tehran and San Francisco have acknowledged the principles of self-determination and equality of nations, will not refuse to acknowledge the independence of Vietnam. . . .

For these reasons, we, members of the Provisional Government of the Democratic Republic of Vietnam, solemnly declare to the world that Vietnam has the right to be a free and independent country—and in fact is so already. The entire Vietnamese people are determined to mobilize all their physical and mental strength, to sacrifice their lives and property in order to safeguard their independence and liberty.

Source: Ho Chi Minh, *Selected Works* (Hanoi: Foreign Languages Publishing House, 1960–1962), 3:17–21.

REVIEW QUESTIONS

How does Ho describe the French political actions in Vietnam?

How does he describe the French economic policies in Vietnam?

Why does he believe the US would support Vietnamese independence?

Jean Monnet, The European Coal and Steel Community, 1953

Seeking peaceful and profitable relations with neighboring countries, France led the way in promoting the economic integration of Western Europe. Foreign Minister Robert Schuman, with American backing, took the first step in May 1950 when he proposed that the coal and steel industries of France and West Germany be placed under a common political authority. Jean Monnet, a prominent French economist, was the driving force behind the proposal to create a common market for coal and steel in Western Europe. In 1951, six countries agreed to establish the European Coal and Steel Community (ECSC), and a year later, Monnet became the first president of the High Authority, the executive body of the supranational organization. Regarded by many as the Father of the European Union, Monnet hoped that the ECSC would be the first step in the gradual political as well as economic unification of Europe. He and other European visionaries looked forward to the eventual creation of a United States of Europe. The excerpts that follow are reproduced from his comments regarding the ECSC made on June 4, 1953, before the US Senate Foreign Relations Committee.

THE UNITED STATES OF EUROPE
These institutions [of the ECSC] are of federal character; in fact, they are the United States of Europe, if you please, in all of its institutional part applying to steel and coal. . . .

THE HIGH AUTHORITY
This High Authority is the executive. What we decide . . . the 6 nations [France, West Germany, Italy, Belgium, Luxembourg, and the Netherlands] have undertaken in their treaty, voted by the 6 parliaments to carry out. . . .

THE ASSEMBLY

Then, there is the Assembly. It is the beginning of a European parliament. It is the first time that there has been in Europe a parliament with delegation of sovereignty from the six nations, and which has effective power. . . .

COURFT OF JUSTICE

Then, the other institution is the Court of Justice. Now, if any government or any interest, steel or coal, in this community feels that the decisions that we have taken are contrary to the treaty and to the powers that have been delegated to us, if we abuse our power or treat our charter wrongly, they can appeal before this Court of Justice. . . .

[A]nd that Court, which is sort of a beginning of the Supreme Court of Europe, when it decides there is no appeal, then all the courts of Europe must carry out the decision and decrees of this Supreme Court. . . .

THE TREATY ON THE COMMUNITY OF COAL AND STEEL

The whole operation of this community is under the special act called the Treaty on the Community of Coal and Steel, which has been submitted and ratified by the 6 parliaments for 50 years, of which one of the main features is the delegation of sovereignty to us as executives, and to the parliament, as the parliament of the community. The parliament controls us and has the right and the duty to dismiss us if they think we are not fulfilling our jobs; they have that right.

SCOPE OF COMMUNITY'S AUTHORITY

You must think of us in terms of the beginning of a United States of Europe. . . . That is what we are and, therefore, what we are doing is—what we have done and what we are actually doing every day, is—the establishment of a common market as if there were no France or Germany or no other countries, for coal and steel.

I mean, imagine that within your United States, if every State of the Union had retained sovereignty, and there was no Washington and Federal authority; there would be one Federal authority for coal and steel so that all matters of coal and steel would be dealt with not according to the law of the separate States but according to a Federal law, and that customs barriers, duties, and all discrimination of any kind would be abolished for these two basic commodities. . . .

PRODUCTION OF COMMUNITY

Let me give you some figures. . . . This community produces at the moment around 40 million tons or so of steel, and 225 million tons of coal. . . . But we think that within the next 5 years or so this community, to meet the needs of Europe and also maintaining its export, should produce about 50 million tons a year of steel; and we have in the matter of coal and coking coal, a special problem. We have the resources, but since 1946 and 1947 this community has constantly imported the balance of its requirements in coking coal from this country [the US]; so much so that in 5 years they have imported more than $2 billion of coking coal from the United States, and in the total deficit of dollars between this country [the US] and Europe this import of coal over the last few years has represented about 20 percent of the total deficit.

Now, we think that one of our major urgent problems is to modernize such mines as can produce small coking coal, to develop the coking ovens—do you say "coke oven"?—so that within the next 4 years or so we could produce out of European resources enough so as to eliminate this deficit in dollars and have enough out of the resources which we possess to meet this growing production of steel in Europe. . . .

DEVELOPMENT OF WESTERN EUROPE
Now, if there is to be the development of Western Europe, and if there is to be a basic fundamental condition for defense, this basic industry must be modernized and increased. There is all the capacity, knowledge, intelligence, and resources, and this development of production is essential not only for the purpose of eliminating the dollar deficit I was talking about, but also to establish the proper basis for this development of Western Europe in relation to Russia, which is absolutely fundamental if we are to maintain Europe on a standard and have it play a greater part in the world than it has, and it can, and must have.

COMPARATIVE PRODUCTION FIGURES
The community produced in 1913, 25 million tons of steel; the United States produced in 1913, 31 million tons of steel; Great Britain 9 million, and Russia alone 4 million. . . . Now, in 1952 we have picked up. We are at 41 million tons, but Russia alone is at 35. Do not forget that we export; and Russia does not, so that the consumption of Russia from those figures, I must say I am surprised myself, is greater than I thought it was in relation to us.

Now, the United States I need not say. It went up to a hundred million; but that gives you the relation. . . .

ULTIMATE HOPES
I think you should realize, at least we believe, in what is the almost inexorable development of this system, the principles, institutions toward a United States of Europe. . . . You must realize there are two things that are now happening

effectively based and springing definitely from this very institution and these very principles and actions, and one is this European army [plans for the establishment of a European Defense Community] which you have heard so much about, and the other one is what is called the political authority.

FIRST DRAFT OF A EUROPEAN CONSTITUTION
The assembly of this community last September was asked by the governments of the six nations to work up the first draft of a constitution for Europe, including a common parliament and a political authority. . . . In other words— this house has begun with a first floor of the coal and steel community, and then came the army in the present treaty, and now comes as the first roof of this first house, a parliament elected by the people, who elect an executive, who would then be responsible for this coal and steel, and the army.

Source: European Coal and Steel Community, Hearings before the Committee on Foreign Relations, United States Senate, Eighty-Third Congress, First Secession, June 4–5, 1953 (Washington, DC: Government Printing Office, 1953), 1–16.

REVIEW QUESTIONS

Why did Monnet believe Western Europe needed to produce more coal and steel?

How did he view the relationship that Western Europe had with the US and the Soviet Union?

What was his goal in advocating the establishment of the ECSC?

Mao Zedong, The Collectivization of Agriculture in China, 1955

The first Five Year Plan in China, launched in 1953, was based on the Soviet economic model. Most of the capital used to fund the rapid development of heavy industry in the cities was extracted from the countryside by forcing peasants to pay high taxes and to sell grain to government stores at low prices fixed by the state. Cheap food permitted low wages for urban workers, thereby leaving more funds for investment in heavy industry. On July 31, 1955, Mao Zedong announced his decision to establish collective farms throughout China at a conference sponsored by the Central Committee of the Chinese Communist Party. Mao emphasized not only the close connection between agricultural collectivization and industrial development but also his determination to promote economic equality in the Chinese countryside. Excerpts from his address on "The Co-operative Transformation of Agriculture" are printed here. Agricultural collectives took possession of the land, tools, and livestock of individual cultivators, and by the end of 1956, more than 90 percent of the rural population of China belonged to collective farms, each comprising about two hundred peasant households.

I.

An upsurge in the new, socialist mass movement is imminent throughout the countryside. But some of our comrades, tottering along like a woman with bound feet, are complaining all the time, "You're going too fast, much too fast." Too much carping, unwarranted complaints, boundless anxiety and countless taboos. . . .

The high tide of social transformation in the countryside, the high tide of co-operation, has already swept a number of places and will soon sweep the whole country. It is a vast socialist revolutionary movement involving a rural population of more than 500 million, and it has tremendous, world-wide significance. We should give this movement active, enthusiastic and systematic leadership, we should not drag it back by whatever means. . . .

II.

The nation-wide co-operative movement is now making tremendous strides forward, and yet we still have to argue such questions as: Can the co-operatives grow? Can they be consolidated? As far as certain comrades are concerned, the crux of the matter seems to be their worry as to whether it is possible to consolidate the several hundred thousand existing semi-socialist co-operatives, which are generally rather small, averaging twenty-odd peasant households each. Of course, unless they can be consolidated, growth is out of the question. . . .

VII.

The great historical experience of the Soviet Union in building socialism inspires our people with full confidence in the building of socialism in China. However, even on this subject of international experience there are different views. Some comrades disapprove of our Central Committee's policy of keeping the development of agricultural co-operation in step with our socialist industrialization, although the validity of such a policy has been borne out in the Soviet Union. While conceding that the speed of industrialization as set at present is all right, they maintain that agricultural co-operation should proceed at an extremely slow pace and need not keep in step. . . . These comrades fail to understand that socialist industrialization cannot be carried out in isolation from the co-operative transformation of agriculture. In the first place, as everyone knows, China's current level of production of commodity grain and raw materials for industry is low, whereas the state's need for them is growing year by year, and this presents a sharp contradiction. If we cannot basically solve the problem of agricultural co-operation within roughly three five-year plans, that is to say, if our agriculture cannot make a leap from small-scale farming with animal-drawn farm implements to large-scale mechanized farming, along with extensive state-organized land reclamation by settlers using machinery . . . , then we shall fail to resolve the contradiction between the ever-increasing need for commodity grain and industrial raw materials and the present generally low output of staple crops, and we shall run into formidable difficulties in our socialist industrialization and be unable to complete it. In the second place, some of our comrades have not given any thought to the connection between the following two facts, namely, that heavy industry, the most important branch of socialist industrialization, produces for agricultural use tractors and other farm machinery, chemical fertilizers, modern means of transport, oil, electric power, etc., and that all these things can be used, or used extensively, only on the basis of an agriculture where large-scale co-operative farming prevails. We are now carrying out a revolution not only in the social system, the change from private to public ownership, but also in technology, the change from handicraft to large-scale modern machine production, and the two revolutions are connected. In agriculture, with conditions as they are in our country, co-operation must precede the use of big machinery. . . . In the third place, some of our comrades have also failed to give any thought to the connection between two other facts, namely, that large funds are needed to accomplish both national industrialization and the technical transformation of agriculture, and that a considerable part of these funds has to be accumulated through agriculture. Apart from the direct agricultural tax, this is done by developing light industry to produce the great quantities of consumer goods needed by the peasants and exchanging them for the peasant's commodity grain and the raw materials for light industry, so that the material requirements of both the peasants and the state are met and funds are accumulated for the state. . . .

IX.

Some comrades take a wrong approach to the vital question of the worker-peasant alliance, proceeding as they do from the stand of the bourgeoisie, the rich peasants, or the well-to-do middle peasants with their spontaneous tendencies toward capitalism. . . . As is clear to everyone, the spontaneous forces of capitalism have been steadily growing in the countryside in recent years, with new rich peasants springing up everywhere and many well-to-do middle peasants striving to become rich peasants. On the other hand, many poor peasants are still living in poverty for shortage of the means of production, with some getting into debt and others selling or renting out their land. If this tendency goes unchecked, it is inevitable that polarization in the countryside will get worse day by day. Those peasants who lose their land and those who remain in poverty will complain that we are doing nothing to save them from ruin or to help them out of their difficulties. . . . Can the worker-peasant alliance hold firm in these circumstances? Obviously not. There is no solution to this problem except on a new basis. And that means to bring about, step by step, the socialist transformation of the whole of agriculture together with socialist industrialization and the socialist transformation of handicrafts and capitalist industry and commerce; in other words, it means to carry out co-operation and eliminate the rich peasant economy and the individual economy in the countryside so that all the rural people will become increasingly well off together. We maintain that this is the only way to consolidate the worker-peasant alliance. Otherwise, this alliance will be in real danger of breaking up. . . .

Source: *Selected Works of Mao Tse-tung* (Peking: Foreign Languages Press, 1978), 5:184–207.

REVIEW QUESTIONS

To whom did Mao address his argument to speed the pace of agricultural collectivization?

How did he view the relationship between agriculture and industry?

How did hope to change the class structure of rural China?

Document 80

Nelson Mandela, I Am Prepared to Die Speech, 1964

The white minority government in South Africa passed discriminatory laws designed to ensure a large supply of cheap Black workers in the countryside. After labor strikes failed to end the system of racial segregation known as apartheid, Nelson Mandela led a sabotage campaign in 1964 in an unsuccessful attempt to overthrow the repressive white regime in Pretoria. Mandela and eight of his colleagues were captured and sentenced to life imprisonment following his statement, excerpted here, given at his trial. Responding to a massive Black protest movement supported by an international economic boycott, the white rules of the pariah nation began to dismantle the apartheid system in 1989. Mandela was set free after spending more than a quarter of a century in prison, and 1994 he became the first Black president of South Africa. Mandela promptly assured the members of the white minority that they would not be mistreated by the Black majority. Although he had been attracted to socialism before his long incarceration, President Mandela embraced free-market policies, which soon led to growing economic inequality within the Black community of South Africa.

South Africa is the richest country in Africa, and could be one of the richest countries in the world. But it is a land of extremes and remarkable contrasts. The whites enjoy what may well be the highest standard of living in the world, whilst Africans live in poverty and misery. Forty per cent of the Africans live in hopelessly overcrowded and, in some cases, drought-stricken Reserves, where soil erosion and the overworking of the soil makes it impossible for them to live properly off the land. Thirty per cent are labourers, labour tenants, and squatters on white farms and work and live under conditions similar to those of the serfs of the Middle Ages. The other 30 per cent live in towns where they have developed economic and social habits which bring

263

them closer in many respects to white standards. Yet most Africans, even in this group, are impoverished by low incomes and high cost of living. . . .

The complaint of Africans, however, is not only that they are poor and the whites are rich, but that the laws which are made by the whites are designed to preserve this situation. There are two ways to break out of poverty. The first is by formal education, and the second is by the worker acquiring a greater skill at his work and thus higher wages. As far as Africans are concerned, both these avenues of advancement are deliberately curtailed by legislation.

The present Government has always sought to hamper Africans in their search for education. One of their early acts, after coming into power, was to stop subsidies for African school feeding. Many African children who attended schools depended on this supplement to their diet. This was a cruel act. . . .

The other main obstacle to the economic advancement of the African is the industrial colour-bar under which all the better jobs of industry are reserved for Whites only. Moreover, Africans who do obtain employment in the unskilled and semi-skilled occupations which are open to them are not allowed to form trade unions which have recognition under the Industrial Conciliation Act. This means that strikes of African workers are illegal, and that they are denied the right of collective bargaining which is permitted to the better-paid White workers. . . .

The lack of human dignity experienced by Africans is the direct result of the policy of white supremacy. White supremacy implies black inferiority. Legislation designed to preserve white supremacy entrenches this notion. Menial tasks in South Africa are invariably performed by Africans. When anything has to be carried or cleaned the white man will look around for an African to do it for him, whether the African is employed by him or not. Because of this sort of attitude, whites tend to regard Africans as a separate breed. They do not look upon them as people with families of their own; they do not realize that they have emotions—that they fall in love like white people do; that they want to be with their wives and children like white people want to be with theirs; that they want to earn enough money to support their families properly, to feed and clothe them and send them to school. And what "house-boy" or "garden-boy" or labourer can ever hope to do this? . . .

Above all, we want equal political rights, because without them our disabilities will be permanent. I know this sounds revolutionary to the whites in this country, because the majority of voters will be Africans. This makes the white man fear democracy.

But this fear cannot be allowed to stand in the way of the only solution which will guarantee racial harmony and freedom for all. It is not true that the enfranchisement of all will result in racial domination. Political division, based on colour, is entirely artificial and, when it disappears, so will the domination of one colour group by another. The ANC [African National Congress] has spent half a century fighting against racialism. When it triumphs it will not change that policy.

This then is what the ANC is fighting. Their struggle is a truly national one. It is a struggle of the African people, inspired by their own suffering and their own experience. It is a struggle for the right to live.

During my lifetime I have dedicated myself to this struggle of the African people. I have fought against white domination, and I have fought against black domination. I have cherished the ideal of a democratic and free society in which all persons live together in harmony and with equal opportunities. It is an ideal which I hope to live for and to achieve. But if needs be, it is an ideal for which I am prepared to die.

Source: Nelson Mandela, Statement given on April 20, 1964 before the Pretoria Supreme Court in South Africa, Nelson Mandela Foundation. https://www.nelsonmandela.org.

REVIEW QUESTIONS

How did Mandela view education?

How did he view labor unions?

Why do you think he was attracted to socialism as a young man?

Document 81

Mikhail Gorbachev, The Quest for Nuclear Disarmament, 1986

During the 1970s, American and Soviet leaders engaged in strategic arms limitation talks in hopes of curbing the expensive arms race and reducing the risk of nuclear war. But their only concrete accomplishment came in May 1972 when Presidents Brezhnev and Nixon signed the Strategic Arms Limitation Treaty (SALT) I, which froze the number of intercontinental ballistic missiles and submarine-based missiles that the US and the Soviet Union could deploy for the next five years. When Ronald Reagan entered the White House in January 1981, he was determined to restore American military supremacy, and soon after referring to the Soviet Union as an Evil Empire in March 1983, he announced his intention to launch a space-based missile defense system to protect the US from the danger of a nuclear attack. On March 11, 1985, however, Reagan sent Mikhail Gorbachev, the new general secretary of the Communist Party of the Soviet Union, a letter indicating a desire to develop a more constructive relationship between their two countries. Reagan also expressed his hope that he and Gorbachev would be able to make progress toward achieving a common goal of eliminating nuclear weapons during a meeting to be held in Geneva. On January 14, 1986, after it became clear that the Reagan intended to build a missile defense system, Gorbachev sent the president a letter, excerpts printed here, that proposed a three-stage procedure for reducing and finally eliminating all nuclear weapons. Although Reagan refused to abandon his commitment to the development of a space-based missile defense system, he did join with Gorbachev in December 1987 in signing a treaty that eliminated only the Soviet and American stockpiles of intermediate land-based missiles that could carry nuclear warheads.

After our meeting in Geneva where we agreed that the questions of security are central for our relations, I have carefully thought through the ways to implement the decisions of principle, which were taken as a result of our meeting. . . .

In your New Year address to the people of the Soviet Union you said that it was your dream to one day free mankind from the threat of nuclear destruction. But why make the realization of this dream conditional on the development of new types of weapons—space weapons in this case? Why take this extremely dangerous path—which does not hold a promise for disarmament, when it is possible already now to get down to freeing the world from existing arsenals?

We propose a different path, which will really enable us to enter the third millennium without nuclear weapons. Instead of spending the next 10–15 years developing new sophisticated weapons in space, which are allegedly intended to make nuclear weapons "obsolete" and "impotent", wouldn't it be better to address those weapons themselves and take that time to reduce them to zero? Let us agree on a stage-by-stage program which would lead to a complete nuclear disarmament everywhere already by the turn of the next century.

The Soviet Union envisages the following procedure of the reduction of nuclear weapons—both delivery vehicles and warheads—down to their complete liquidation.

The first stage. It would last approximately [sic] 5–8 years. During this period the USSR and US would reduce by half their nuclear weapons reaching the territories of each other. There would remain no more than 6000 warheads on the delivery vehicles still in their possession.

It goes without saying that such reductions take place on the basis of the mutual renunciation by the USSR and US of the development testing and deployment of attack space weapons. As the Soviet Union has repeatedly warned, the development of space weapons will dash the hopes for reductions of nuclear weapons on Earth.

The Soviet Union, as is known, has long been proposing that Europe be freed from nuclear weapons, both medium range and tactical. We are in favor of reaching and implementing already at the first stage a decision to eliminate completely the medium range missiles of the USSR and US in the European zone—both ballistic and cruise missiles—as the first step towards freeing the European continent from nuclear weapons. In this context, naturally, the US would have to assume the obligation not to transfer its strategic and medium range missiles to other countries, and Britain and France—not to build up their corresponding nuclear weapons.

From the outset, in our view, it is necessary for the USSR and US to agree to cease all nuclear explosions and to call upon other states to join such moratorium as soon as possible. I shall return to this issue later.

The second stage. It has to start no later than 1990 and last 5–7 years. Britain, France and China start to join nuclear disarmament. To begin with they could assume the obligation to freeze all their nuclear armaments and not to have them on the territories of other countries.

The USSR and US continue the reduction on which they agreed at the first stage and carry out further measures to liquidate their medium range nuclear weapons, and freeze their tactical nuclear systems. After the USSR and US complete the reduction by 50 percent of their relevant armaments, another radical step is taken—all nuclear powers liquidate their tactical nuclear weapons, that is, systems with ranges (radius of action) of up to 1000 kilometers.

At this stage the Soviet-American agreement to ban attack space weapons must become multilateral, necessarily involving all leading industrial powers.

All nuclear powers would cease nuclear testing.

A prohibition would be introduced on the development of non-nuclear weapons based on new physical principles, which by their destructive capabilities come close to nuclear or other systems of mass destruction.

No later than 1995 the third stage will start. During this stage the liquidation of all still remaining nuclear weapons is completed. By the end of 1999 no more nuclear weapons remain on Earth. A universal agreement is worked out that these weapons shall never be resurrected again.

It is envisaged that special procedures will be worked out for the destruction of nuclear weapons as well as for the dismantling, conversion or destruction of their delivery vehicles. In this context agreement will be reached on the quantities of weapons to be destroyed at each stage, the places where they will be destroyed etc.

The verification of the weapons destroyed or limited would be carried out by both national technical means and by on-site inspection. The USSR is prepared to come to terms on any other additional verification measures.

All this'll become possible if we close the way for the arms race in outer space. I would like to hope, that you, Mr. President, will consider this question with all the attention it deserves.

Source: Mikhail Gorbachev to Ronald W. Reagan, January 14, 1986. These materials are reproduced from www.nasrchive.org with the permission of the National Security Archive.

REVIEW QUESTIONS

What steps did Gorbachev propose for the first stage of nuclear disarmament?

What steps did he propose for the second stage?

What was his goal with respect to nuclear weapons?

Document 82

Deng Xiaoping, Reform Policies in China, 1987

Deng Xiaoping, who became the paramount leader of China in November 1978, was determined to maintain the dictatorial power of the Chinese Communist Party while adopting policies that would generate economic development, even if the result would be increased social inequality. Believing in the need for material incentives, Deng dismantled agricultural collectives and permitted peasant households to sell their crops for a profit, and he allowed factory workers to be paid according to their job performance. Deng also opened China to an inflow of foreign capital and technology. During a talk with Stefan Korosec, a Communist leader from Yugoslavia, Deng explained his desire to speed up the program of economic reform in China and to accelerate the policy of opening the country to the outside world. Excerpts from the conversation, which took place on June 12, 1987, are printed here.

China is now carrying out a reform. I am all in favor of that. There is no other solution for us. After several decades of practice it turned out that the old ways didn't work. We used to copy foreign models mechanically, which only hampered the development of our productive forces, induced ideological rigidity and kept the people and grass-roots units from taking any initiative. We made some mistakes of our own as well, such as the Great Leap Forward and the "cultural revolution," which were our own inventions. I would say that since 1957 our major mistakes have been "Left" ones. The "cultural revolution" was an ultra-Left mistake. In fact, during the 20 years from 1958 through 1978, China was hesitating, virtually at a standstill. There was little economic growth and not much of a rise in the standard of living. How could we go on like that without introducing reforms? So in 1978, at the Third Plenary Secession of the Eleventh Central Committee, we formulated a new basic political line: to give first priority to the drive for modernization and strive to develop the productive forces. In accordance with that line, we drew up a series of new principles and policies, the major ones being reform and the open policy. By reform we mean something comprehensive, including reform of both the economic structure and the political structure and corresponding changes in all other areas. By the open policy we mean opening to all other countries, irrespective of their social systems.

We introduced reform and the open policy first in the economic sphere, beginning with the countryside. Why did we start there? Because that is where 80 percent of China's population lives. An unstable situation in the countryside would lead to an unstable political situation throughout the country. If the peasants did not shake off poverty, it would mean that China remained poor. Frankly, before the reform the majority of the peasants were extremely poor, hardly able to afford enough food, clothing, shelter and transportation. After the Third Plenary Session of the Eleventh Central Committee, we decided to carry out rural reform, giving more decision-making power to the peasants and the grass-roots units. By so doing we immediately brought their initiative into play, and great changes took place. By diversifying agriculture in accordance with local conditions, the peasants have grown grain and cash crops in places suited to them and have substantially increased the output of both. . . .

Our success in rural reform increased our confidence, and, applying the experience we had gained in the countryside, we began a reform of the entire economic structure, focused on the cities.

In the meantime, we have implemented the policy of opening China to the outside world in many ways, including setting up special economic zones and opening 14 coastal cities. . . .

The Shenzhen Special Economic Zone has achieved remarkable success since it was established almost eight years ago. . . . The people of Shenzhen reviewed their experience and decided to shift the zone's economy from a domestic orientation to an external orientation, which meant that Shenzhen would become an industrial base and offer its products on the world market. It is only two or three years since then, and already the situation in Shenzhen has changed greatly. The comrades there told me that more than 50 per cent of their products were exported and that receipts and payments of foreign exchange were in balance. . . .

Now a new question has been raised, reform of the political structure. . . . The democracy in capitalist societies is bourgeois democracy—in fact, it is the democracy of monopoly capitalists. It is no more than a system of multiparty elections, separation of judicial, executive and legislative powers and a bicameral legislature. Ours is a system of people's congresses and people's democracy under the leadership of the Communist Party; we cannot adopt the practice of the West. The greatest advantage of the socialist system is that when the central leadership makes a decision, it is promptly implemented without interference from any other quarters. When we decided to reform the economic structure, the whole country responded; when we decided to establish special economic zones, they were soon set up. We don't have to go through a lot of discussion and consultation, with one branch of government holding up another and decisions being made but not carried out. From this point of view, our system is very efficient. The efficiency I am talking about is overall efficiency. We have superiority in this respect, and we should keep it—we should retain the advantages of the socialist system.

In terms of administrative and economic management, the capitalist countries are more efficient than we in many respects. China is burdened with bureaucratism. Take our personnel system, for example, I think the socialist countries all have a problem of aging cadres, so that leaders at all levels tend to be rigid in their thinking. . . .

In general, old people tend to be conservative. They all have one thing in common: they consider problems only in the light of their personal experience. In today's world things are moving with unprecedented rapidity, especially in science and technology. . . . We must keep abreast of the times; that is the purpose of our reform. We must firmly carry out the policy of promoting younger leading cadres, but we must be cautious. And we should not regard youth as the only criterion for promoting cadres. They should have political integrity and professional competence, broad experience and familiarity with conditions, so that they will form an echelon of leaders of different ages. . . .

In short, so far as economic reform is concerned, the principles, policies and methods have been set. All we have to do now is to speed up their implementation. As for reform of the political structure, it is still under discussion. . . .

Source: *The Selected Works of Deng Xiaoping* (Beijing: Foreign Languages Press, 1897), 3:234–40.

REVIEW QUESTIONS

Why did the economic reform program in China begin in the countryside?

Where did the Shenzhen Special Enterprise Zone sell its industrial products?

How did Deng assess the efficiency of China compared to the capitalist countries?

Document 83

Osama bin Laden, A Declaration of Jihad against the United States, 1996

In a speech delivered to his al-Qaeda followers in Afghanistan in August 1996, Osama bin Laden called upon Muslims to conduct a holy war to drive Americans out of Saudi Arabia. Mecca and Medina, the two most revered Islamic cities, are both located in Saudi Arabia. Muhammad, the prophet who founded Islam was born in Mecca, the home the Ka'ba, the holiest Muslim shrine. In 622 CE, Muhammad and his followers fled from Mecca to Medina, where they lived according to Sharia law, a legal code based on Islamic beliefs and practices. Bin Laden's declaration of Jihad against the US was audiotaped for worldwide distribution. Excerpts taken from his fatwa are printed here. On September 11, 2001, al-Qaeda carried out high-profile attacks on the World Trade Center and the Pentagon, symbols of American economic and military power. The US and several other Western nations promptly dispatched troops to Afghanistan to stop al-Qaeda from using that country as a terrorist base. On May 2, 2011, American special forces killed Bin Laden in Pakistan, and on August 30, 2021, the US completed the withdrawal of its troops from Afghanistan as al-Qaeda was reestablishing its terrorist network in that country.

The people of Islam awakened and realized that they are the main target for the aggression of the Zionist-Crusaders alliance. All false claims and propaganda about "Human Rights" were hammered down and exposed by the massacres that took place against the Muslims in every part of the world.

The latest and the greatest of these aggressions experienced by the Muslims since the death of the Prophet is the occupation of [Saudi Arabia] the land of the two Holy Places—the foundation of the house of Islam, the place of the revelation, the source of the message and the place of the noble Ka'ba. . . .

People [in Saudi Arabia] are fully concerned about their everyday living; everybody talks about the deterioration of the economy, inflation, ever increasing debts and jails full of prisoners. . . .

The crusader forces became the main cause of our disastrous condition, particularly in the economical aspect of it due to the unjustified heavy spending on these forces. As a result of the policies imposed on the country, especially in the oil industry where production is restricted or expanded and prices are fixed to suit the American economy, ignoring the economy of the country. Expensive deals were imposed on the country to purchase arms. . . .

The [Saudi] regime is fully responsible for what has been incurred by the country and the nation; however the occupying American enemy is the principle and the main cause of the situation. Therefore efforts should be concentrated on destroying, fighting and killing the enemy until, by the Grace of Allah, it is completely defeated. . . .

It is incredible that our country is the world's largest buyer of arms from the USA and the area's biggest commercial partner of the Americans who are assisting their Zionist brothers in occupying Palestine and in evicting and killing Muslims there, by providing arms, men and financial support.

To deny these occupiers the enormous revenues from their trade with our country is a very important help for our Jihad against them. To express our anger and hate to them is a very important moral gesture. By doing so we would have taken part in cleansing our sanctities from the Crusaders and the Zionists and forcing them, by the Permission of Allah, to leave disappointed and defeated.

We expect the women of the land of the two Holy Places and other countries to carry out their role in boycotting American goods.

If economic boycott is intertwined with the military operations of the Mujahideen [holy warriors], then defeating the enemy will be even nearer, by the Permission of Allah. . . .

I say: Since the sons of the two Holy Places feel and strongly believe that fighting against the Kuffar [nonbelievers] in every part of the world is absolutely essential; then they would be even more enthusiastic, more powerful and larger in number upon fighting on their own land—the place of their births—defending the greatest of their sanctities, the noble Ka'ba. They know that the Muslims of the world will assist and help them to victory. To liberate their sanctities [Holy Places] is the greatest issue concerning all Muslims; it is the duty of every Muslim in this world. . . .

Those youths know that their reward in fighting you, the USA, is double than their reward in fighting someone else not from the book [believers in the Koran]. They have no intention except to enter paradise by killing you. . . .

Those youths are different from your soldiers. Your problem will be how to convince your troops to fight, while our problem will be how to restrain our youths to wait their turn in fighting. . . .

Source: Osama bin Laden, Declaration of War Against the Americans Occupying the Land of the Two Holy Places, August 23, 1996 http://web .archive.org/web/20100812060339/ and http://www.pbs.org/newshour /terrorism/international/fatwa_1996.html. [The text of this fatwa, first published in *Al Quads Al-Arabi* in August 1996, was reprinted online by the PBS News Hour and copyrighted in 2001 by Mac Neil-Lehrer Productions.]

REVIEW QUESTIONS

Who did Bin Laden blame most for conditions in Saudi Arabia?

What action did he want Saudi women to take against Americans?

Why did he believe that young Saudi men would fight vigorously against Americans?

Document 84

Condoleezza Rice, Asia-Pacific Economic Integration, 2006

In January 2007, the Socialist Republic of Vietnam became the 150th member of the World Trade Organization. The Asia-Pacific Economic Cooperation (APEC) summit had been held just two months earlier in Hanoi, the Vietnamese capital. On November 18, 2006, Condoleezza Rice, the US secretary of state, delivered a keynote address to business executives attending the APEC meeting. Excerpts from her remarks, which are printed here, reveal the American desire for the creation on an Asia-Pacific Free Trade Area. Nearly ten years later on February 4, 2016, representatives from the US and eleven other countries signed the Trans-Pacific Partnership (TTP) a multilateral agreement designed to expand trade across a vast region. But the US Congress, reflecting fears that the deal would lead to a decline in American manufacturing, did not ratify the TTP. Although the US formally withdrew from the TTP in January 2017, the eleven other TPP countries signed a slightly modified version of the pact and left the door open for the US to rejoin the trade organization.

Fellow ministers, distinguished guests, ladies and gentlemen: it is my great pleasure to join all of you here in Hanoi for this year's APEC summit. The United States views APEC as the premier multilateral organization in the Asia-Pacific region. And here in this room today, we see the true spirit of APEC—in people like you, and millions of other entrepreneurs across Asia-Pacific, who work every day to create jobs, to expand opportunity, and to unleash the energy of the imagination of the Asia-Pacific community.

The United States has always been a Pacific power, and we are proud to support and be part of Asia's success. We have opened our markets to Asia's entrepreneurs. We have opened our schools and universities to Asia's students. . . . In 1989, we and our Asian partners joined together to create this great organization, APEC.

The results of our cooperation have been dramatic: Since the creation of APEC, the combined wealth of our economies has grown by 66 percent. Today, nearly two-thirds of all U.S. trade occurs with our friends in the Asia-Pacific. And the benefits on this side of the ocean are plain for all to see: People in this region are lifting themselves out of poverty, in greater numbers and with greater speed, than ever before in human history.

The lesson, ladies and gentlemen, is clear: The economies of the Asia-Pacific region are completely and inextricably linked together. We share the benefits, as well as the burdens, of expanding prosperity. For this reason, APEC, and the free economies of the Asia-Pacific, should know that they have no better friend, and no stronger supporter, than the United States of America.

Today, I would like to share America's vision for APEC with you. It is a vision that transcends simple cooperation, and looks to the emergence of a true Asia-Pacific Economic Community, spanning the public sphere and the private sector. I see several principles that must define that sense of community.

We must create opportunities for sustainable growth. There is simply no better way to achieve this goal than free trade, and the United States has a comprehensive trade policy in Asia-Pacific. . . .

We are working with our APEC partners and with you in the business community to promote regional economic integration, including the possibility of a Free Trade Area of the Asia-Pacific. . . .

Our sense of economic community must promote well-governed societies. Just as APEC is increasingly recognizing that prosperity depends on security, we are also acknowledging the connection between development and good governance. More and more entrepreneurs are sick and tired of bearing the economic risks of political malfeasance—and for good reason. Who wants to do business in an economy where the rule of law is enforced by whim or perhaps not at all? Or of where the state is compromised by corruption? Or where the intellectual products of innovation can be pirated at any cost?

This is an area in which we must work together, because corruption and the absence of the rule of law will most certainly retard economic growth, both for growing, developed economies and also for those who wish to enter the international economic system and gain benefit and prosperity for their people.

Finally, our sense of economic community must strengthen our shared institutions. On this front, the United States will lead by example. Over the next two years, President Bush plans to increase America's funding for APEC—to empower this organization to meet the challenges of the 21st century. . . .

Source: Condoleezza Rice, Remarks at the APEC CEO Summit, Hanoi, November 18, 2006, US State Department Archive http://2001-2009.state .gov/secretary/rm/2006/76277.htm.

REVIEW QUESTIONS

How did Rice think trade benefitted the members of APEC?

How did she envision the future of the Asia-Pacific region?

How did she view the importance of rules governing commerce?

Document 85

Nadege Rolland, China's Belt and Road Initiative, 2018

After Xi Jinping became the president of China in 2013, he pursued the overarching goal of national rejuvenation. Determined to make his country prosperous and powerful as it had been in the past, Xi declared that China should double its per capita gross domestic product from 2010 to 2020 and establish a strong military capable of fighting and winning wars. Xi launched two major initiatives in hopes of achieving his economic and strategic objectives. In 2013, he announced the Belt and Road Initiative designed to revive the ancient silk roads that stretched overland and across the seas. And in 2015, he announced the Made in China 2025 Initiative, aimed at achieving rapid economic growth in key areas such as aerospace, robotics, electric vehicles, and information technology. Nadege Rolland, a senior fellow at the National Bureau of Asian Research, provided a penetrating analysis of the Belt and Road Initiative. Excerpts of her testimony, presented to the US-China Economic and Security Review Commission, on January 25, 2018, appear here.

The Belt and Road Initiative (BRI) is generally understood as China's plan to finance and build infrastructure projects across Eurasia. Infrastructure development is in fact only one of BRI's five components which include strengthened regional political cooperation, unimpeded trade, financial integration and people-to-people exchanges. Taken together, BRI's different components serve Beijing's vision for regional integration under its helm. It is a top-level design for which the central government has mobilized the country's political, diplomatic, intellectual, economic and financial resources. It is mainly conceived as a response to the most pressing internal and external economic and strategic challenges faced by China, and as an instrument at the service of the PRC's vision for itself as the uncontested leading power in the region in the coming decades. As such, it is a grand strategy.

1. Belt and Road: What is It? The Belt and Road Initiative was not an-
    nounced as such five years ago, but in two separate speeches given by
    Xi Jinping: the first in Astana in September 2013, announcing China's
    willingness to create a Silk Road Economic Belt stretching across land
    from China to Europe; the second in Jakarta in October 2013, men-
    tioning China's desire to launch its equivalent at sea, the 21st Century
    Maritime Silk Road. Both proposals rapidly got combined under the
    abbreviation "One Belt, One Road," an English translation officially
    replaced in 2015 by "Belt and Road Initiative" (BRI), supposedly to
    counter the impression that China owned the concept and to reflect
    its willingness to welcome others' participation. The basic idea is that
    infrastructure building (roads, railways, port facilities, pipelines, fiber
    optic and IT networks) across Eurasia will bring economic develop-
    ment to a large region spanning East to West from China's eastern
    shores to Europe via Russia, Central Asia, South Asia and the Middle
    East, and from China's southern shores to Southeast Asia, the Indian
    ocean rim, the Persian Gulf and the Mediterranean. This is a vast re-
    gion mainly composed of emerging markets and rising middle classes
    and which, taken together, accounts for two thirds of the world popula-
    tion and over half of the global GDP. . . . Sparing no modesty for a plan
    he personally designed with a handful of close advisors, Xi Jinping
    hailed BRI as the "project of the Century." If successful, BRI certainly
    has the potential to fundamentally change the economic and strategic
    geography of the region.
2. What Purpose Does It Serve? Even though BRI is officially portrayed
    and projected outside China as an economic endeavor that is meant
    for the benefit of the entire region, the internal discussions related to
    the project reveal it is mostly intended to serve China's interests and
    objectives, both in the economic and strategic domains.
    *   *On the economic side,*
        BRI should be understood, at least partly, as a new stimulus pack-
        age for the Chinese economy whose last double-digit growth was
        recorded in 2010. Right after the 2008 global financial crisis, the
        Chinese government quickly launched a $586 billion stimulus
        package, heavily investing in domestic infrastructure projects in
        order to help sustain growth. This measure only had a short-lived
        positive effect. The government needed to find another solution to
        be able to hit its self-imposed target of doubling GDP and per capita
        income between 2010 and 2020. From the regime perspective
        though, a thorough transformation of the country's economic devel-
        opment model towards domestic consumption and private initiative

would have come at unacceptable political cost. Instead of veering towards such a transformation, the government decided to rely once again on its preferred model, stimulating growth through investment, exports and subsidies to state-owned enterprises (SOEs), operating outside of China on a regional scale, via BRI.

Building infrastructure across Eurasia would also have the double advantage of helping to get rid of some of China's excess industrial capacity that had been created by the 2008 stimulus package, while further supporting the state conglomerates' "going global" strategy. Funded by Chinese policy banks (Eximbank, China Development Bank) and staffed by Chinese workers, regional infrastructure projects would predominantly become the preserve of China's SOEs (China State Construction Engineering, China Railway Construction, State Grid, China Merchants, etc.), opening new markets for them and helping them build and scale a truly global footprint. Finally, it was hoped that BRI would help increase regional e-commerce and cross-border transactions conducted in renminbi, thus accelerating the Chinese currency's internationalization.

- *Beyond the supposed multiple economic gains BRI would bring to China, its architects also believe it will help reap substantial political and geostrategic benefits for their country.*

First among these, and consistent with what the Chinese Communist Party (CCP) has tried to do for almost two decades albeit with uneven results, the hope is that more investment in regional infrastructure will help reduce the development gap between China's coastal and inner provinces. Sandwiched between its own eastern urbanized dynamic coastal poles, and emerging economies with increasing potential outside of its western and southern borders, China's landlocked provinces lag behind in term of economic development. Development and enhanced living standards are seen by Beijing as key factors to reduce the risk of social unrest and political instability. They are also seen as the best ways to discourage religious radicalization, fundamentalism, and terrorist recruitment—both within China's borders and beyond.

Second, the acceleration of investments in infrastructure induced by BRI would enable Beijing to tackle another of its recurrent anxieties, this time related to its energy security. For years, Beijing has been uneasy at the thought that its energy imports transit through sea lanes of communication that are under the protection and surveillance of the U.S. Navy including in the South China Sea. Beijing has been looking for alternative routes to circumvent the so-called "Malacca Strait dilemma" and diversify its supplies through land routes. The projected and current BRI projects illustrate an attempt to redraw the map of China's energy supply routes from Iran, the Gulf countries and eastern Africa, while increasing its imports from Russia and Central Asia. Traveling by sea/land pipelines through Pakistan and Myanmar, or directly by land across Eurasia, some of China's energy imports would thus bypass the South China Sea, reducing the risk of being cut by a potential American naval blockade in case of a military conflict.

Lastly, China's financial, political and diplomatic investment in BRI does not come out of a heartfelt Chinese commitment to serve the common good. In return for its largess, China expects to get some concrete geopolitical benefits for itself. BRI's architects are blurring the lines between economy and strategy, and intend to use economic power as an instrument for strategic purposes. Instead of gunboat diplomacy and coercive military power, the PRC intends to use BRI to access new markets, get a hold on to critical infrastructure assets, and influence regional countries' strategic decisions. Economic leverage will be used both as an incentive to garner support for its interests and reduce potential resistance, and as a means to punish recalcitrant countries.

Beijing expects that its plan will help "expand its circle of friends"—in other words, strengthen its influence in a vast area where democratic practice is weak, authoritarian regimes mostly prevail, and where the US influence is rather limited. In this region, as in countries facing increasing waves of discontent against globalization, there is a real prospect that following the "China model" could become increasingly appealing. Liberal democratic ideals and standards that the U.S., together with its European and Asian allies, have been trying to promote over the region as part of their shared post-Cold War vision of an "open and free" Eurasian continent, will likely come under increasing threat as BRI's standards (or lack thereof) spread across this vast region.

Under Xi Jinping, China has been increasingly vocal about its dissatisfaction with the current world order. During his 19th Party Congress speech last October, Xi presented China's path as "a new option for other countries and nations who want to speed up their development while preserving their independence." Starting with the countries included along the Belt and Road that Xi purports to include in a "community of common destiny," the PRC now offers a recipe for stability and prosperity, just like the one it has used for itself, and it is trying to convince the rest of the world that the Chinese way is the way of the future.

3. Internal Mobilization

   BRI is meant to improve both China's economic situation and its security environment in order to realize Xi Jinping's "China dream of the great rejuvenation of the nation." It is the organizing concept of Xi's vision for China as a rising global power with unique national characteristics. . . . As such, it is a grand strategy that is meant to serve China's unimpeded rise to great power status.

Source: Hearing on China's Belt and Road Initiative: Five Years Later, Before the U.S.-China Economic and Security Commission, Washington DC, January 25, 2018. This document is available via: www.uscc.gov.

REVIEW QUESTIONS

In what ways is the BRI intended to benefit China economically?

How is the BRI intended to serve the geopolitical interests of China?

How does the BRI dovetail with the Made in China 2025 Initiative?

Vladimir Putin, On the Historical Unity of Russians and Ukrainians, 2021

After becoming president of Russia in 2000, Vladimir Putin had a long-range goal: He wanted to reestablish the Russian Empire as it stood in 1917 before the Bolsheviks replaced the tsarist autocracy with a socialist regime. Putin was serving as a KGB agent in 1991 when the Union of Soviet Socialist Republics (USSR) disintegrated, and by 2004 several East European countries that were previously dominated by the Soviet Union had joined both the European Union (EU) and North Atlantic Treaty Organization (NATO). Regarding the breakup of the USSR as the greatest geopolitical catastrophe of the twentieth century, Putin viewed the eastward expansion of the EU and NATO as a direct threat to his dream of making Russia a global power as it had been in the past. Putin aimed to establish a strong economic and military bloc stretching across the vast Eurasian landmass from Poland to the Pacific, and he was determined to gain control of Ukraine, an important agricultural and industrial country that was central to his imperial ambitions. In 2014, Putin dispatched troops to seize the Crimean Peninsula, a Ukrainian province that was formerly part of the Soviet Union and home to its Black Sea fleet. And a few months later, after he annexed the Crimea, Putin sent troops to support a separatist rebellion in the Donbas region of eastern Ukraine. Putin launched a full-scale invasion of Ukraine on February 24, 2022, in hopes of establishing a puppet government in Kyiv and extinguishing the independence of the country. His essay "On the Historical Unity of Russians and Ukrainians," published on July 12, 2021, and excerpted here, can be seen as a justification for a future Russian military assault on Ukraine.

First of all, I would like to emphasize that the wall that has emerged in recent years between Russia and Ukraine, between the parts of what is essentially the same historical and spiritual space, to my mind is our great common misfortune and tragedy. These are, first and foremost, the consequences of our own mistakes made at different periods of time. But these are also the result of deliberate efforts by those forces that have always sought to undermine our unity. The formula they apply has been known from time immemorial—divide and rule. There is nothing new here. Hence the attempts to play on the "national question" and sow discord among people, the over-arching goal being to divide and then to pit the parts of a single people against one another. . . .

Russians, Ukrainians, and Belarusians are all descendants of Ancient Rus, which was the largest state in Europe. Slavic and other tribes across the vast territory—from Ladoga, Novgorod, and Pskov to Kiev and Chernigov—were bound together by one language (which we now refer to as Old Russian), economic ties, the rule of the princes of the Rurik dynasty, and—after the baptism of Rus—the Orthodox faith. The spiritual choice made by St. Vladimir, who was both Prince of Novgorod and Grand Prince of Kiev, still largely determines our affinity today.

The throne of Kiev held a dominant position in Ancient Rus. This had been the custom since the late 9th century. . . .

Later, like other European states of that time, Ancient Rus faced a decline of central rule and fragmentation. At the same time, both the nobility and the common people perceived Rus as a common territory, as their homeland. . . .

Most importantly, people both in the western and eastern Russian lands spoke the same language. Their faith was Orthodox. Up to the middle of the 15th century, the unified church government remained in place. . . .

In the second half of the 18th century, following the wars with the Ottoman Empire, Russia incorporated Crimea and the lands of the Black Sea region, which became known as Novorossiya. They were populated by people from all of the Russian provinces. After the partitions of the Polish-Lithuanian Commonwealth, the Russian Empire regained the western Old Russian lands, with the exception of Galicia and Transcarpathia, which became part of the Austrian—and later Austro-Hungarian—Empire.

The incorporation of the western Russian lands into the single state was not merely the result of political and diplomatic decisions. It was underlain by the common faith, shared cultural traditions, and—I would like to emphasize it once again—language similarity. . . .

In 1922, when the USSR was created, with the Ukrainian Soviet Socialist Republic becoming one of its founders, a rather fierce debate among the Bolshevik leaders resulted in the implementation of Lenin's plan to form a union state as a federation of equal republics. The right for the republics to freely secede from the Union was included in the text of the Declaration on the Creation of the Union of Soviet Socialist Republics and, subsequently, in the

1924 USSR Constitution. By doing so, the authors planted in the foundation of our statehood the most dangerous time bomb, which exploded the moment the safety mechanism provided by the leading role of the CPSU was gone, the party itself collapsing from within. A "parade of sovereignties" followed. On 8 December 1991, the so-called Belovezh Agreement on the Creation of the Commonwealth of Independent States was signed, stating that "the USSR as a subject of international law and a geopolitical reality no longer existed." By the way, Ukraine never signed or ratified the CIS Charter adopted back in 1993.

In the 1920's–1930's, the Bolsheviks actively promoted the "localization policy," which took the form of Ukrainization in the Ukrainian SSR. . . .

The localization policy undoubtedly played a major role in the development and consolidation of the Ukrainian culture, language and identity. At the same time, under the guise of combating the so-called Russian great-power chauvinism, Ukrainization was often imposed on those who did not see themselves as Ukrainians. This Soviet national policy secured at the state level the provision on three separate Slavic peoples: Russian, Ukrainian and Belorussian, instead of the large Russian nation, a triune people comprising Velikorussians, Malorussians and Belorussians.

In 1939, the USSR regained the lands earlier seized by Poland. A major portion of these became part of the Soviet Ukraine. . . . In 1954, the Crimean Region of the RSFSR was given to the Ukrainian SSR, in gross violation of legal norms that were in force at the time. . . .

The Bolsheviks treated the Russian people as inexhaustible material for their social experiments. They dreamt of a world revolution that would wipe out national states. That is why they were so generous in drawing borders and bestowing territorial gifts. It is no longer important what exactly the idea of the Bolshevik leaders who were chopping the country into pieces was. We can disagree about minor details, background and logics behind certain decisions. One fact is crystal clear: Russia was robbed, indeed. . . .

Of course, inside the USSR, borders between republics were never seen as state borders; they were nominal within a single country, which, while featuring all the attributes of a federation, was highly centralized—this, again, was secured by the CPSU's leading role. But in 1991, all those territories, and, which is more important, people, found themselves abroad overnight, taken away, this time indeed, from their historical motherland. . . .

When the USSR collapsed, many people in Russia and Ukraine sincerely believed and assumed that our close cultural, spiritual and economic ties would certainly last, as would the commonality of our people, who had always had a sense of unity at their core. However, events—at first gradually, and then more rapidly—started to move in a different direction.

In essence, Ukraine's ruling circles decided to justify their country's independence through the denial of its past, however, except for border issues. They began to mythologize and rewrite history, edit out everything that united us, and refer to the period when Ukraine was part of the Russian Empire and the Soviet Union as an occupation. The common tragedy of collectivization and famine of the early 1930s was portrayed as the genocide of the Ukrainian people.

Radicals and neo-Nazis were open and more and more insolent about their ambitions. They were indulged by both the official authorities and local oligarchs, who robbed the people of Ukraine and kept their stolen money in Western banks, ready to sell their motherland for the sake of preserving their capital. To this should be added the persistent weakness of state institutions and the position of a willing hostage to someone else's geopolitical will.

I recall that long ago, well before 2014, the U.S. and EU countries systematically and consistently pushed Ukraine to curtail and limit economic cooperation with Russia. We, as the largest trade and economic partner of Ukraine, suggested discussing the emerging problems in the Ukraine-Russia-EU format. But every time we were told that Russia had nothing to do with it and that the issue concerned only the EU and Ukraine. De facto Western countries rejected Russia's repeated calls for dialogue.

Step by step, Ukraine was dragged into a dangerous geopolitical game aimed at turning Ukraine into a barrier between Europe and Russia, a springboard against Russia. . . .

Nor were the interests of the Ukrainian people thought of in February 2014. The legitimate public discontent, caused by acute socio-economic problems, mistakes, and inconsistent actions of the authorities of the time, was simply cynically exploited. Western countries directly interfered in Ukraine's internal affairs and supported the coup. Radical nationalist groups served as its battering ram. Their slogans, ideology, and blatant aggressive Russophobia have to a large extent become defining elements of state policy in Ukraine.

All the things that united us and bring us together so far came under attack. . . .

But the fact is that the situation in Ukraine today . . . involves a forced change of identity. And the most despicable thing is that the Russians in Ukraine are being forced not only to deny their roots, generations of their ancestors but also to believe that Russia is their enemy. It would not be an exaggeration to say that the path of forced assimilation, the formation of an ethnically pure Ukrainian state, aggressive towards Russia, is comparable in its consequences to the use of weapons of mass destruction against us. As a result of such a harsh and artificial division of Russians and Ukrainians, the Russian people in all may decrease by hundreds of thousands or even millions. . . .

The anti-Russia project has been rejected by millions of Ukrainians. The people of Crimea and residents of Sevastopol made their historic choice. And people in the southeast peacefully tried to defend their stance. Yet, all of them, including children, were labeled as separatists and terrorists. They were threatened with ethnic cleansing and the use of military force. And the residents of Donetsk and Lugansk took up arms to defend their home, their language and their lives. . . .

This is what is actually happening. First of all, we are facing the creation of a climate of fear in Ukrainian society, aggressive rhetoric, indulging neo-Nazis and militarizing the country. Along with that we are witnessing not just complete dependence but direct external control, including the supervision of the Ukrainian authorities, security services and armed forces by foreign advisers, military "development" of the territory of Ukraine and deployment of NATO infrastructure. . . .

Again, for many people in Ukraine, the anti-Russia project is simply unacceptable. And there are millions of such people. But they are not allowed to raise their heads. They have had their legal opportunity to defend their point of view in fact taken away from them. They are intimidated, driven underground. Not only are they persecuted for their convictions, for the spoken word, for the open expression of their position, but they are also killed. Murderers, as a rule, go unpunished. . . .

All the subterfuges associated with the anti-Russia project are clear to us. And we will never allow our historical territories and people close to us living there to be used against Russia. And to those who will undertake such an attempt, I would like to say that this way they will destroy their own country. . . .

Russia is open to dialogue with Ukraine and ready to discuss the most complex issues. But it is important for us to understand that our partner is defending its national interests but not serving someone else's, and is not a tool in someone else's hands to fight against us. . . .

I am confident that true sovereignty of Ukraine is possible only in partnership with Russia. Our spiritual, human and civilizational ties formed for centuries and have their origins in the same sources, they have been hardened by common trials, achievements and victories. Our kinship has been transmitted from generation to generation. It is in the hearts and the memory of people living in modern Russia and Ukraine, in the blood ties that unite millions of our families. Together we have always been and will be many times stronger and more successful. For we are one people. . . .

Source: The website of the President of the Russian Federation, www
.kremlin.ru

REVIEW QUESTIONS

Why does Putin view Russians and Ukrainians as one people?

What role does he believe that religion played uniting these people?

What does he think the Bolsheviks did to undermine the unity of Russians and Ukrainians?

What does he believe that foreigners did to divide these people?

Bibliography

"A Look at the Situation of the Peasant Question at the Present Time (August 1859)." Russkii arkiv (Russian Archive), 1869, vyp. (issue) 8, 1364–76.

A Sourcebook for Russian History from Early Times to 1917. Vol. 1, Early Times to the Late Seventeenth Century, edited by George Vernadsky et al. (New Haven, CT: Yale University Press, 1972), 246–47.

al-Din, Rashid. *Compendium of Chronicles.* Translated by Wheeler Thackston (Cambridge, MA: Harvard University Department of Near Eastern Languages and Civilizations, 1998).

An Arab Philosophy of History: Selections from the Prolegomena of Ibn Khaldūn. Edited and translated by Charles Issawi. (London: John Murray, 1950), 68–70, 78, 80–81.

Archer, T. A., ed. *The Crusade of Richard I* (New York: G. P. Putnam's Sons, 1889), 127–31.

Aristotle's Politics. Translated by Benjamin Jowett (Oxford: Clarendon Press, 1920), 114–16, 149, 162, 168–69.

Bill of Rights. UK Parliament, 1689.

bin Laden, Osama. Declaration of War Against the Americans Occupying the Land of the Two Holy Places. 23 August 1996 http://web.archive.org/web/20100812060339 /http://www.pbs.org/newshour/terrorism/international/fatwa_1996.html

Boston Commercial Bulletin, 5 October 1867, 8.

British Foreign Policy, 1919–1939, 2nd Series. 1939, VII:258–60.

British Parliamentary Papers. Reports from Committees, vol. 15 (London: House of Commons).

Bruel, Alexandre, ed. "Recueil des Chartes de L'Abbaye de Cluny." (Paris: Imprimerie Nationale, 1876). Quoted in Ernest F. Henderson, trans., *Select Historical Documents of the Middle Ages* (London: George Bell and Sons, 1910), 329–33.

Bryan, William Jennings, ed. *The World's Famous Orations* (New York: Funk and Wagnalls, 1906), 4:60–70.

China in Transition, 1517–1911. Translated by Dan J. Li (New York: Van Nostrand Reinhold Company, 1969), 6–7.

Dodgeon, Michael H., and Samuel N. C. Lieu, eds. *The Roman and Eastern Frontier and the Persian Wars (AD 226–363): A Documentary History.* (London: Routledge, 1991), 57, 58, 61.

Ebrey, Patricia Buckley, ed. *Chinese Civilization: A Sourcebook*, revised and expanded edition. Translated by Chiu-yueh Lai (New York: Free Press, 1993, 1981), 112–15.

Ebrey, Patricia Buckley, ed. and trans. *Chinese Civilization: A Sourcebook*, revised and expanded edition (New York: Free Press, 1993, 1981), 116–19.

Ebrey, Patricia Buckley. ed. *Chinese Civilization: A Sourcebook*, 2nd ed., revised and expanded. Translated by Clara Yu. (New York: Free Press, 1993), 178–85. Original source: "Duzheng jisheng," in *Dongjing Menghua lu, wai si zhong* (Shanghai: Zhonghua shuju, 1962), 91–101.

Ehrenberg, Richard. *Capital and Finance in the Age of the Renaissance: A Study of the Fuggers and Their Connections*, trans. H. M. Lucas (New York: Augustus M. Kelley, 1963), 80.

European Coal and Steel Community. Hearings before the Committee on Foreign Relations, United States Senate, 83rd Congress, First Secession, 4–5 June 1953 (Washington, DC: Government Printing Office, 1953), 1–16.

Ferry, Jules. *Le Tonkin et la Mere-Patrie* (Paris: Victor-Harvard, 1890), 40–43, 47–48.

Fontaine, James. *Memoirs of a Huguenot Family.* Edited by Ann Maury. (New York: G. P. Putnam and Company, 1853), 351–52.

Foreign Relations of the United States: The Lansing Papers (Washington, DC: Government Printing Office, 1939), 1:144–47.

Foster, C. T., and F. H. Blackburne Daniell. "Süleyman the Lawgiver" in *The Life and Letters of Ogier Ghiselin de Busbecq* (London: Hakluyt Society, 1881), 1:152–56.

Han Feizi: Basic Writings. Translated by Burton Watson. (New York: Columbia University Press, 2003), 21, 22, 24, 28, 29.

Harper, Robert F., ed. *Assyrian and Babylonian Literature: Selected Translations* (New York: D. Appleton and Company, 1901), 118–24.

Harper, Robert F., ed. and trans. *The Code of Hammurabi* (Chicago, IL: University of Chicago Press, 1904), 3–109.

Hearing on China's Belt and Road Initiative: Five Years later, Before the U.S.-China Economic and Security Commission. Washington, DC, January 25, 2018. Available at: www.uscc.gov.

Hearings Before the Special Committee Investigating the Munitions Industry, 74th Cong., 2d. Sess., pt. 26 (Washington, DC: Government Printing Office, 1937), 8123–25.

Henderson, Ernest F., trans. and ed. *Select Historical Documents of the Middle Ages* (London: George Bell and Sons, 1892), 165–67.

Hill, John E. "A Translation of the Kharosthi Documents from Chinese Turkestan." Silk Road Seattle, https://depts.washington.edu/silkroad/texts/niyadocts.html. Translation from A. M. Boyer et al., *Discovered by Sir Aurel Stein in Chinese Turkestan* (Oxford: Clarendon Press, 1920).

Ho Chi Minh. *Selected Works* (Hanoi: Foreign Languages Publishing House, 1960–1962), 3:17–21.

Hobson, John A. *Imperialism: A Study* (London: James Nesbit and Co., 1902). The excerpts are taken from Chapter VI, titled The Economic Taproot of Imperialism, 76–99.

Hopkins, J. F. P. trans. *Corpus of Early Arabic Sources for West African History*. Edited by J. F. P. Hopkins and Nehemia Levtzion. (Cambridge: Cambridge University Press, 1981), 79–80.

Howard, Dick, ed. *Selected Political Writings, Rosa Luxemburg*. Monthly Review Press, 1971.

Joseph, Gilbert M., and Timothy J. Henderson. *The Mexican Reader: History, Culture, and Politics* (Durham, NC: Duke University Press, 2002), 339–43.

Keen, Benjamin, ed. and trans. *Latin American Civilization*, 3rd ed. (Boston, MA: Houghton Mifflin, 1974), 1:19–22.

Ku, Pan. *The History of the Former Han Dynasty*. Vol. 3. A Critical Translation with Annotations by Homer H. Dubs with the collaboration of Jen T'ai and P'an Lo-chi. [The American Council of Learned Societies.] (Baltimore: Waverly Press, 1938).

Langdon, S., and Alan Gardiner. "The Treaty of Alliance between Hattusili, King of the Hittites, and Pharaoh Ramesses II of Egypt." Translated by A. H. Gardiner. *The Journal of Egyptian Archaeology*, 6, no. 3 (July 1920): 179–205.

Legge, James, ed. and trans. *The Chinese Classics* (London: Henry Frowde, 1893), 4:171–72.

"Letters from the Kings of the Kongo to the King of Portugal." *Monumenta Missionaria Africana*, ed. Antonio Brasio, (Lisboa: Agencia Geral do Ultramar, 1952), 1:262–63, 294–95, 335, 404, 470, 488.

Malthus, Thomas. *An Essay on the Principle of Population* (London: Printed for J. Johnson, in St. Paul's Church-Yard, 1798), 3–10.

Mandela, Nelson. Statement given on 20 April 1964 before the Pretoria Supreme Court in South Africa. Nelson Mandela Foundation. https://www.nelsonmandela.org.

Markham, Clements R., trans. and ed. *The Travels of Pedro de Cieza de Leon, A.D. 1532–1550, Contained in the First Part of his Chronicle of Peru* (London: Hakluyt Society, 1864), 144–50.

Medieval Trade in the Mediterranean World. Edited by Robert Lopez and Irving Raymond. Number LII of the *Records of Civilization Sources and Studies Series*, edited by Austin P. Evans. (New York: Columbia University Press, 1955), 176–77.

Melmoth, W., trans. *The Letters of Pliny the Consul* (London: J. Dodsley, 1770), 2:595–98, 610–14, 620–24.

Miller [Mueller], G. F. *Storiia Sibiri*. (Moscow: AN SSSR, 1937–1941), 1: 333.

Moyle, J. B., ed. *The Institutes of Justinian*, 5th ed. (Oxford: Oxford University Press, 1913).

Mun, Thomas. *England's Treasure by Forraign Trade* (New York: Macmillan and Company, 1895).

National Security Archive. Mikhail Gorbachev to Ronald W. Reagan, 14 January 1986. These materials are reproduced from www.nasrchive.org with the permission of the National Security Archive.

Observation Touching on the Trade and Commerce with the Hollanders, and Other Nations. (London: William Sheeres, 1653). Reprinted in *Sources of the Western Tradition.* Vol. 1, 4th ed., eds. Marvin Perry, Joseph R. Peden and Theodore H. Von Laue (Boston, MA: Houghton Mifflin), 341–43.

Okuma, Count Shigenobu, ed. *Fifty Years of New Japan*, 2nd ed. [English version edited by Marcus B. Huish.] (London: Smith, Elder & Co., 1910), I: 479–82.

Paine, Thomas. *Rights of Man: Being an Answer to Mr. Burke's Attack on the French Revolution* (London: J. M. Dent & Sons, Ltd., 1915), 94–97.

Plutarch's Lives: The Translation Called Dryden's Corrected from the Greek and Revised by A. H. Clough (Chicago, IL: University of Chicago Press, 1868), IV:506–30. [The present translation, originally published in 1683–1686 by John Dryden, was revised in 1864 by Arthur H. Clough.]

Plutarch's Lives: The Translation Called Dryden's Corrected from the Greek and Revised by A. H. Clough (Boston, MA: Little Brown & Co., 1868), I:168–202. [The present translation, originally published in 1683–1686 by John Dryden, was revised in 1864 by Arthur H. Clough.]

Postelthwayt, Malachy. *The National and Private Advantages of the African Trade Considered.* (London: John and Paul Knapton, 1746).

Quranic Arabic Corpus. Maintained by the quran.com team. This is an open source project. The Quranic Arabic Corpus is available under the GNU public license with terms of use.

Readings in European History. Edited by James Harvey Robinson (Boston, MA: Ginn and Company, 1904), 30–33.

Rice, Condoleezza. Remarks at the APEC CEO Summit, Hanoi, 18 November 2006. US State Department Archive http://2001-2009.state.gov/secretary/rm/2006/76277.htm

Richardson, James D., ed., *Messages and Papers of the Presidents* (New York: Bureau of National Literature, Inc., 1897), I:205–16.

Robinson, James Harvey, ed. *Readings in European History* (Boston, MA: Ginn & Company, 1904), 1:178–80.

Sandars, Thomas Collett, trans. and ed. *The Institutes of Justinian* (New York: Longman's, Green, and Co., 1917), 1–7.

Sansom, Sir George Bailey. *A History of Japan* (Stanford, CA: Stanford University Press, 1963), III:99.

Savory, Roger M., trans. *Eskander Bey Monshi: History of Shah Abbas the Great* (Boulder, CO: Westview Press, 1978), 1:523, 527–29, 531, 533.

Schoff, Wilfred H., trans. and ed. *The Periplus of the Erythraean Sea: Travel and Trade in the Indian Ocean by a Merchant of the First Century* (New York: Longmans, Green, and Co., 1912).

Select Historical Documents of the Middle Ages. Translated by E. F. Henderson (London: George Bell and Sons, 1892), 176–89.

Selected Works of Mao Tse-tung. (Peking: Foreign Languages Press, 1978), 5:184–207.

Smith, Vincent A. *Asoka: The Buddhist Emperor of India* (Oxford: Clarendon Press, 1901), 129–33.

Sources of Chinese Tradition. Edited by William Theodore de Bary and Irene Bloom (New York: Columbia University Press, 1999), 1:363–66.

Sources of Chinese Tradition, 2nd ed. Compiled and translated by William Theodore de Bary and Irene Bloom. (New York: Columbia University Press, 1999), 1:360–63.

Sources of the Western Tradition, vol. 1, 4th ed. Edited by Marvin Perry, Joseph R. Peden and Theodore H. Von Laue (Boston: Houghton Mifflin).

Speeches and Writings of M. K. Gandhi, 3rd ed. (Madras: G A. Natesan & Co., 1922), 751–57.

Sun Tzu on the Art of War: The Oldest Military Treatise in the World. Translated by Lionel Giles. (London: Luzac & Co., 1910), 6–30.

The Book of Ser Marco Polo, the Venetian, Concerning the Kingdoms and Marvels of the East, 3rd ed. Translated by Henry Yule. (London: John Murray, 1903), 423–26.

The Chinese Repository. Vol. VIII, No. 10 (February 1840), 497–503.

The Domesday Survey of Chester. Edited and translated by James Tait (Manchester: Chetham Society, 1916), pp. 79–87.

The Geography of Strabo. Literally translated, with notes, in three volumes. (London. George Bell & Sons. 1903), Book VXII, Chapter 1.

"The Life of Augustus," in *The Lives of the Twelve Caesars.* Translated by J. C. Wolfe (London: Loeb Classical Library, 1913).

The Selected Works of Deng Xiaoping (Beijing: Foreign Languages Press, 1897), 3:234–40.

The Theodosian Code. Edited and translated by Clyde Pharr (Princeton, NJ: Princeton University Press, 1952), 287–88.

The Travels of Ibn Battuta. A.D. 1325–1354. Translated and edited by H. A. R. Gibb (London: Hakluyt Society, 1962), II:373–82.

The website of the President of the Russian Federation: www.kremlin.ru.

Thucydides. *The History of the Peloponnesian War.* Translated by Richard Crawley. (London: J. M. Dent and Company, 1903), 243–48.

Translations and Reprints from the Original Sources of European History, vol VI, no. 5 (Philadelphia: The Department of History of the University of Pennsylvania, 1899), 16–27.

US House of Representatives. Hearings before the Subcommittee on Foreign Trade and Shipping, Special Committee on Post-War Economic Policy and Planning, 79th Congress 1st Session (Washington: Government Printing Office, 1945), 1972–98.

US National Parks Service. Declaration of Sentiments. Available at: https://www.nps .gov/wori/learn/historyculture/declaration-of-sentiments.htm.

Van Doren, Carl, and Julian P. Boyd, eds. *Indian Treaties Printed by Benjamin Franklin 1736–1762* (Philadelphia: Historical Society of Pennsylvania, 1938), 75.

Vsepoddanneishii doklad ministra finansov S. Iu. Vitte Niklaiu II o neobkhodimosti ustanovit' i zatem neprelozhno priderzhivat'sia opredelennoi programmy torgovo-promyshlennoi politiki imperii. GA RF fond 601, opis' 1, delo 1026, listy 1–12. [This document from the Russian archives in Moscow has been translated for us by Professor Douglas R. Weiner of the University of Arizona.]

Yule, Henry, and Henri Cordier, trans. and ed. *Cathay and the Way Thither, Being a Collection of Medieval Notices of China* (London, 1916), III:143–71.

SPEECHES

Selected Political Writings, Rosa Luxemburg. Edited and introduced by Dick Howard. Monthly Review Press © 1971. Translated: Rosmarie Waldrop (from the German Ausgewählte Reden und Schriften, 2 (Berlin: Dietz Verlag, 1951, pp. 433–41). Transcription/Markup: Brian Baggins. Copyright: Monthly Review Press © 1971. Published here by the Marxists Internet Archive (marxists.org, 2003) with permission from Monthly Review Press.

Index

About the Authors

James R. Farr received his PhD from Northwestern University and then taught a variety of classes for nearly forty years at the University of Tennessee and Purdue University. A specialist in European and World History, he has authored eight and edited two books. Most recently he coauthored with Patrick J. Hearden a world history textbook, *Wealth, Power, and Inequality in World History*, 2 vols. (Cognella, 2022). He retired in 2021 and lives in West Lafayette, Indiana, and Sarasota, Florida, with his wife Danielle and his dog Louie.

Patrick J. Hearden, professor emeritus of history, Purdue University, is a snowbird who spends summers in Illinois and winters in Arizona. After receiving his PhD at the University of Wisconsin–Madison, Hearden spent most of his academic career teaching undergraduate and graduate courses in US History and World History. Over the years, he has written several books dealing with US foreign relations. In his most recent publication, Hearden joined with James R. Farr to coauthor a two-volume textbook, *Wealth, Power, and Inequality in World History* (Cognella, 2022).